Challenging Inclusive Education Policy and Practice in Africa

Studies in Inclusive Education

Series Editors

Roger Slee (*University of South Australia, Australia*)

Editorial Board

Mel Ainscow (*University of Manchester, UK*)
Felicity Armstrong (*Institute of Education, University of London, UK*)
Len Barton (*Institute of Education, University of London, UK*)
Suzanne Carrington (*Queensland University of Technology, Australia*)
Joanne Deppeler (*Monash University, Australia*)
Linda Graham (*Queensland University of Technology, Australia*)
Levan Lim (*National Institute of Education, Singapore*)
Missy Morton (*University of Canterbury, New Zealand*)

VOLUME 40

The titles published in this series are listed at *brill.com/stie*

Challenging Inclusive Education Policy and Practice in Africa

Edited by

Sulochini Pather and Roger Slee

BRILL
SENSE

LEIDEN | BOSTON

All chapters in this book have undergone peer review.

Library of Congress Cataloging-in-Publication Data

Names: Pather, Sulochini, editor. | Slee, Roger, editor.
Title: Challenging inclusive education policy and practice in Africa / edited
  by Sulochini Pather and Roger Slee.
Description: Leiden ; Boston : Brill Sense, [2019] | Series: Studies in
  inclusive education ; volume 40 | Includes bibliographical references.
Identifiers: LCCN 2018049056 (print) | LCCN 2018051822 (ebook) | ISBN
  9789004391505 (E-Book) | ISBN 9789004391482 (paperback) | ISBN
  9789004391499 (hardback)
Subjects: LCSH: Inclusive education--Africa. | Inclusive
  education--Government policy--Africa. | Education and state--Africa.
Classification: LCC LC1203.A35 (ebook) | LCC LC1203.A35 C53 2019 (print) |
  DDC 371.9/046096--dc23
LC record available at https://lccn.loc.gov/2018049056

Typeface for the Latin, Greek, and Cyrillic scripts: "Brill". See and download: brill.com/brill-typeface.

ISSN 2542-9825
ISBN 978-90-04-39148-2 (paperback)
ISBN 978-90-04-39149-9 (hardback)
ISBN 978-90-04-39150-5 (e-book)

Copyright 2019 by Koninklijke Brill NV, Leiden, The Netherlands.
Koninklijke Brill NV incorporates the imprints Brill, Brill Hes & De Graaf, Brill Nijhoff, Brill Rodopi,
Brill Sense, Hotei Publishing, mentis Verlag, Verlag Ferdinand Schöningh and Wilhelm Fink Verlag.
All rights reserved. No part of this publication may be reproduced, translated, stored in a retrieval system,
or transmitted in any form or by any means, electronic, mechanical, photocopying, recording or otherwise,
without prior written permission from the publisher.
Authorization to photocopy items for internal or personal use is granted by Koninklijke Brill NV provided
that the appropriate fees are paid directly to The Copyright Clearance Center, 222 Rosewood Drive, Suite
910, Danvers, MA 01923, USA. Fees are subject to change.

This book is printed on acid-free paper and produced in a sustainable manner.

Contents

List of Figures and Tables   VII
Notes on Contributors   VIII

Introduction: Exploring Inclusive Education and 'Inclusion' in the
African Context   1
    Sulochini Pather and Roger Slee

1 Challenging Inclusive Education Policy and Practice in Libya   15
    Abdelbasit Gadour

2 Strides and Strains in Including Children with Disabilities
in Rwandan Education: Critical Reflections on Disability,
Policies and Practice in Education Developments   31
    Evariste Karangwa

3 Towards Inclusive Education Development: Addressing the
Gap between Rhetoric and Practice in Zanzibar Schools   51
    Said Juma

4 Inclusive Education Policy and Practice in Ghana: Air Castle
or Realistic Goal?   69
    William Nketsia

5 In Search of an Inclusive Pedagogy in South Africa   87
    Sigamoney Manicka Naicker and Sindiswa Stofile

6 Special and Inclusive Education Policy and Practice in Kenya, 1963 to 2016:
The Journey   104
    Martin Mwongela Kavua

7 In-Service Tutor Development in Support of Inclusive Education:
Lessons from Partnerships between University and Organizations   118
    Lawrence Eron

8 Inclusive Education Policy Implementation in Swaziland:
   A Critical Reflection on Developments Since 2011   130
       Cebsile P. Nxumalo

9 Challenges of Implementing Inclusive Education and Supporting
   Marginalized Groups in Ethiopia   148
       Ali Sani Side

Figures and Tables

Figures

5.1 Maslow's hierarchy of needs (from Burleson & Thoron, 2014, reprinted with permission).   95

7.1 Training session for braille writing and reading.   125

7.2 Training session for sign language.   125

Tables

7.1 Evolution of the school aged population, 2010–2025.   121

7.2 Beneficiaries.   122

7.3 Participant characteristics.   123

7.4 Topics covered.   124

Notes on Contributors

Lawrence Eron
is a Senior Lecturer at the Faculty of Special Needs and Rehabilitation of Kyambogo University. He is an Education and Development practitioner with vast experience in Primary, Special Needs and Inclusive Education, Teacher Education and Development Studies. For the last 22 years, he has been involved in teacher education, training, research and advocacy for the inclusion of children and young adults with disabilities. Dr. Eron has coordinated many academic and development projects on disability, special needs teacher training and inclusive education. He initiated and chaired the Institutional Disability Policy for Kyambogo University to ensure Disability Inclusion in Higher Education. His research interest focuses on deaf education, inclusive teacher education and rehabilitation science.

Abdelbasit Gadour
is the Cultural Attaché of the Libyan Embassy UK. Over the last couple of years he directed and managed the scholarship scheme of over five thousand students from Libya, studying full time in UK universities. He is also a member of the academic staff at Omar Al-Mukhtar University, Libya. He has trained and worked as an educational psychologist in the UK where he coordinated various projects concerned with children experiencing special educational needs. His expertise in this field and child/educational psychology has led him to carry out intensive research both in Libya and the UK. He is also a member of the editing team of the *Mediterranean Journal of Educational Studies* (MJES).

Said Juma
is an Assistant lecturer in the School of Education, State University of Zanzibar, Tanzania. He is currently a Doctoral candidate (from 2014) in the Faculty of Education, University of Jyvaskyla, Finland. His research interests include inclusive education development, educational action research, teacher continuing professional development, sociology of education and guidance and counselling in educational settings.

Evariste Karangwa
is the founding Dean of the School of Inclusive & Special Needs Education at the University of Rwanda-College of Education (UR CE). He pioneered the integration of students with disabilities in the country, after the genocide against Rwandan Tutsi of 1994. He obtained his M.ED. and Ph.D. from the University of Birmingham (UK) and Catholic University of Louvain (Belgium) respectively.

He has occupied various academic leadership responsibilities in UR CE, and has led teams that reviewed the National Policy on Inclusive Education (2013); the UR policy and guidelines on inclusive teaching and learning (2015); and the Academic Quality Guidelines for Students with Special Seeds (2017) for the Inter University Council of East African (IUCEA). He is the Chief Editor of the *Rwandan Journal of Education*, has published in the *International Journal of Inclusive Education*, the *International Journal of Disability & Development* and others.

Martin Mwongela Kavua

is a Ph.D. student at Kenyatta University in Nairobi, Kenya. He holds a Joint Masters degree in Special and Inclusive Education from Roehampton University (UK); Oslo University (NO); and Charles University in Prague (CZ). His other qualifications include a Bachelor of Education (Special Education) degree from Kenyatta University in Nairobi, Kenya, as well as a primary teacher certificate among other qualifications. He is a lecturer in the department of hearing impairment and communication difficulties at the Kenya Institute of Special Education (KISE) in Nairobi Kenya. Kavua has done consultancy work for various government, non-governmental institutions and Universities in Kenya on various areas including Kenyan Sign Language, special and inclusive education, disability mainstreaming, and disability policy issues as well as Information Communication Technology (ICT) in Education. His publications include the book *Communication Strategies for Deaf Learners in Inclusive Settings* (2014) and a teacher-training manual on Inclusive Education. He has presented papers in various conferences and workshops in the country and internationally. He is also a member of the National Technical Committee on the Digital Learning Programme in Kenya.

Sigamoney Manicka Naicker

is Chief Director Inclusive Education in the Western Cape, Cape Town, South Africa. He has written widely and was the first director of inclusive education in South Africa. He has helped write and launch the 'Education White Paper 6 on Special Needs Education: Building an Inclusive Education in South Africa'. Sigamoney has written widely and has spoken in various forums both locally in South Africa and internationally. Sigamoney is a keen athlete and has run the New York, London, Oslo and Cape Town Marathons.

William Nketsia

is a PhD student at the University of Jyväskylä, Finland. His research interests include inclusive education, implementation of inclusive education, teacher preparation for inclusive education and inclusive pedagogy. William has an extensive teaching experience in primary and secondary schools in Ghana and United Kingdom and University level in Finland. He obtained his Bachelor's Degree in Science Education at the University of Cape Coast, Ghana and his Master's Degree in Education at University of Jyväskylä, Finland.

Cebsile P. Nxumalo

is a Special Needs and Inclusive Education Quality Assurance Officer in the Ministry of Education and Training in the Kingdom of Eswatini. She has played a very significant role in providing leadership and strategic planning for special and inclusive education in the Kingdom of Eswatini for the past 19 years and has also contributed to development of inclusive education at SADC level. She is a member of the Steering Committee for the newly founded Africa Network of Inclusive Education (ANIE). She has worked as a part-time lecturer in the department of Special and Inclusive Education at the Southern Africa Nazarene University in Swaziland (SANU). She was also part of the team that was responsible for developing the Special Needs and Inclusive Education degree programmes offered at SANU. She is a researcher and has published a number of papers in international journals. Her latest paper "Financing of Inclusive Education in Urban Settings of Swaziland" was published in the *Second International Handbook of Urban Education* in 2017.

Sulochini Pather

is a Full Professor of Inclusive Education at Nazarbayev University Graduate School of Education. She is originally from South Africa, but has lived and worked as Principal and Senior Lecturer at several universities in the UK and elsewhere for the past 19 years. She is an international reviewer on the *International Journal of Inclusive Education* and the *Asia Journal of Inclusive Education*. She is the Founder and Chair of the Africa Network of Inclusive Education (ANIE). She was formerly the Director for Inclusive Education in the National Ministry of Education in South Africa and Lead Consultant for the Finnish Consulting Group on an inclusive education project, working alongside the Ministry of Education in Ethiopia. Her book *Inclusive Education in the Developing World* is due to be released in July 2019.

Ali Sani Side

is lecturer and researcher at Dilla University, Ethiopia, where he has been since 2011. From 2013 to 2015, he served as head of department, special needs and inclusive education and as leader for higher diploma program in Dilla University. He also served as National Advisor for Inclusive Education Master Plan for Ethiopia in a bilateral project between the Federal Democratic Republic of Ethiopia, Ministry of Education and The Government of Finland.

He also contributed to the development of school standards for the Ministry of Education, Ethiopia. He received a B.Ed. and M.Ed. in Special Needs Education from Addis Ababa University and is currently pursuing his Ph.D. in Special Needs Education from Addis Ababa University. His research interests are inclusive education, special needs education, stress related to parenting children with disabilities, academic stress of students with disabilities, the education of children with emotional and behavioral disorder and the different stress coping strategies. Mr. Side is co-author of an article on academic stress and coping strategies among students with disabilities in Addis Ababa University, in the *Eastern Africa Social Science Research Review.*

Roger Slee

holds the Crossing the Horizon Chair in Education at the University of South Australia. He is also a Visiting Professor at the Centre for Disability Studies in the School of Sociology and Social Policy at The University of Leeds. He is the Founding Editor of *The International Journal of Inclusive Education* (Taylor & Francis) and *The Journal of Disability Studies in Education* (Brill). He was formerly the Chair of Inclusive Education at The Institute of Education – UCL and Deputy Director-General of the Queensland Ministry of Education. His latest book is called *Inclusive Education Isn't Dead, It Just Smells Funny* (2018).

Sindiswa Stofile

is a senior lecturer in the Department of Psychology at the University of the Western Cape. She taught in primary and secondary schools for 10 years and in a Teacher College of Education for 15 years. She coordinated a National Department of Basic Education inclusive education pilot project in the Eastern Cape. She specialises in special and inclusive education with her main focus on literacy and numeracy. She has worked individually with learners experiencing difficulties in reading and mathematics and provides consultancy support and in-service training to teachers on barriers to learning in a range of educational settings.

INTRODUCTION

Exploring Inclusive Education and 'Inclusion' in the African Context

Sulochini Pather and Roger Slee

1 Background

'We don't have inclusive education because we don't have special schools'. This was a response to a question of what inclusive education looked like in Seychelles from a conference delegate in 2006. This statement is reflective of several positions. The first is that inclusive education is only about children with disabilities and special needs, which is the mandate of special schools worldwide. The second is that inclusive education is viewed in the same way as special education; that without special education, you cannot have inclusive education. This suggests that in order for inclusive education to work, you would need knowledge and skills in special education and 'special educational needs children'. This notion of inclusive education is prevalent in the African context. In this book, the authors collectively unravel and challenge this common set of assumptions.

On offer is a rethinking of a notion of Inclusive Education in the African context in relation to the underpinning notion of 'inclusion' within unique contexts. We argue that local definitions of inclusion push the boundaries of inclusive education in this continent, to embracing the diversity of learners and their identities of gender, language, race and ethnicity, class, sexuality, (dis)ability, and tribal and religious affiliations. The key question is: how can the values espoused by local notions of inclusion be put into practice to ensure that sites of learning acknowledge and tap into the knowledge, histories and cultures of learners to benefit learning for all? In this respect, we acknowledge the leadership provided by UNESCO (2016) in its honoring of geo-political specificity to achieve the aspirations of *Education for All* (UNESCO, 2015, 2017).

Inclusive Education as an international movement has grown from simply focusing on mainstreaming children with disabilities, which was given impetus at a conference in Salamanca in 1994 (UNESCO, 1994). The focus internationally has widened to being about curriculum, pedagogy and inclusive school development for *all l*earners, not just children with disabilities (Croll & Moss, 2000). The focus in countries in Africa however, has been about increasing

© KONINKLIJKE BRILL NV, LEIDEN, 2019 | DOI:10.1163/9789004391505_001

numbers of children with 'special needs and disabilities' into regular schools, believing that they have been moving towards inclusive education (Phasha et al., 2017; Armstrong et al., 2000). This has in itself not been an easy road.

In this book, we offer local insights into other African countries, building on the recent Phasha, Mahlo, and Dei (2017) text on Inclusive Education in Africa. The countries represented in our text have been chosen as a result of academic associations with the authors, not as a selective country sample. However, these do represent the North and South of the continent. The chapters we include in this book are written by local voices, in recognition that these are the most appropriate people to present the realities as it is seen through local eyes and voiced. This book includes insights from African authors; African being defined as people born in Africa or 'people who have ancestral connection to the African continent' (Njoroge, 2004, p. 223). What better way than to let African authors tell their stories so it isn't diluted by outsiders.

We have chosen to write about Africa, given our work experience in this continent, our interest and because little is written about Inclusive Education in this continent (e.g. Mariga et al., 2014; Muthukrishna, 2008). Literature in the field has been dominated by authors from the North, writing about developments and thinking in the North. Books on Inclusive Education in Africa are also predominantly written by authors from the North, albeit a limited number of titles (e.g. Armstrong et al., 2000; Barton & Armstrong, 2007; Mitchell, 2005). The most recent book written on Inclusive Education in Africa offers valuable local insights (Phasha, Mahlo, & Dei, 2017).

We begin by looking at what Inclusive Education means; internationally and in the African continent, and the tensions in relation to a local African concept of 'inclusion' and the values associated with these meanings. Collectively the authors identify the barriers encountered in putting these values into action and how these barriers are being addressed in different countries?

2   Inclusive Education

There is no one definition of inclusive education. It is not a single movement, but 'made up of many strong currents of belief, many different local struggles and myriad of practice' (Cough & Corbett, 2000, p. 6). For many, inclusion is solely about children with disabilities and about where and how to support them in the education system (Davis, 2003; Fox, 2004). For others, it's about the psycho-medical aspects of individual difference, pathologising difference, which has been a recurrent focus since the 50s (Healy, 2011; Kauffman & Hallahan, 1995; Kauffman & Sasso, 2006). Children with disabilities were the concern for doctors, psychiatrists, educational psychologists and other medical practitioners according to this view of individual defectiveness. In contrast, there has also been a growing emphasis on sociological perspectives and how society contributes to the invention of special needs and disability as socially constructed (Oliver, 1990; Oliver & Barnes, 2012; Boronski & Hassan, 2015). Others focus on curricular approaches: what curriculum and strategies are needed to support special needs (Tomlinson, 2016; Brownell & Smith, 2012). The most compelling focus is on school reform led by inclusive values to accommodate diversity (Slee, 2010, 2018; Booth & Ainscow, 2016). Fundamentally, principles of equality and social justice underwrite the inclusive education script. It is unequivocally a political education manifesto.

Despite the many and competing definitions of inclusive education, there is consensus that it is a fundamental right for all children to be given access to quality education to ensure they reach their full potential as individuals; a right which is reflected in international law in Article 26 of the Universal Declaration of Human Rights and supported by the Education for All Agenda (1990) and the United Nations Convention on the Rights of People with Disabilities and Optional Protocol (2006). Nation states across Africa have signed up to these protocols and remain committed to ensuring education for all children. The progress globally however in the past 25 years, including in Africa, has been slow (UNESCO, 2015).

One of the reasons for this slow progress is that the inclusion of children with disabilities is seen as a separate agenda and support for this is often left to a separate department within Ministries of Education and to the work of NGOs, Disabled People's Organisations and other community organisations working on the ground. This is a result of Africa's colonial past. It is also the residue of the enduring influence of traditional special education in Ministries of Education. In the latter half of the nineteenth century, Christian missionary zeal from Britain was directed to Africa for the establishment of native education (Whitehead, 2015). With it came the establishment of schools for children with disabilities, namely the Deaf and Blind. Joseph Kisanji (1998) from Tanzania suggested that 'the move towards inclusive education in relation to people with disabilities is a Western realization of the problems brought about by 'bundling PWDs up' in asylums and later in special schools, a system which was transported wholesale to countries of the South'. (Kisanji, 1998, p. 55). It resonates with arguments put forward by international and comparative education critiques on how information is shared or rather transported from North to South without deeper reflection on appropriateness or sustainability for local contexts (Pather & Nxumalo, 2012; Phillips & Schweisfurth, 2008; Crossely & Watson, 2008). One legacy of colonialism is a deeply entrenched belief that 'West knows best' (Alur, 2007, p. 98). Neo-colonialism has replaced colonialism with models of practice in inclusive education being imported from the West, namely the UK and the USA, mostly by postgraduates studying in foreign contexts (Gadour, 2007). Hegemony around knowledge on inclusive education radiates from the West.

There is a common tension in the way governments view inclusive schools. Often inclusive education and inclusive schooling is seen as including children in a mainstream school but with separate provision. Other challenges to inclusive education in Africa include lack of teacher training, lack of physical accessibility, lack of resources and materials, inflexible curriculum, pedagogy and assessment (McConkey & Bradely, 2010; Eleweke & Rodda, 2002). A bleak picture is painted by Armstrong et al. (2010) who suggest that implementation of inclusive education in Africa is particularly difficult given the cycle of economic and health poverty due to the effects of colonialism, international loans, lack of access to basic services, etc. (Armstrong, Armstrong, & Barton, 2010). There has been a growth in student numbers in Sub-Saharan Africa, but no increase in the number of teachers resulting in increased student-teacher ratios, large class sizes and insufficient resources at best (Armstrong, Armstrong, & Barton, 2010). This is exacerbated by limited or no teacher training, to deal with children with disabilities.

The other challenge is the dominant view of disability. Indigenous knowledge and perceptions of disability vary across the African continent, although much of the evidence suggests a predominantly negative view based on cultural beliefs, which leads to discrimination (Eide, 2014). Some believe it is a punishment from God (Waliaula, 2009). Parents often also believe that their children with disabilities cannot be educated, which prevents them from sending them to school.

Poverty is often considered a key contributor to disability in Africa. However, a review of the relationship between poverty and disability indicated a cross section between poverty and disability, but there is no evidence of causal relationships (Eide, Khupe, & Mannan, 2014). The review also indicated the lack of disability-specific and awareness data, which is excluded from socio-economic planning processes.

3 Inclusion

Again, definitions of inclusion are multifarious and often in opposition with each other (Slee, 2018). Inclusion as a philosophical concept fundamentally presupposes democracy and implies equal relationships (Young, 2002). It is an unambiguous rejection of exclusion (Slee, 2011), which is underpinned by a commitment to human rights. However, many like Croll and Moss (2000) suggest inclusion in education occupies a 'moral high ground' and is unachievable, while others like Kauffman and Hallahan (1995) and Farrell (2006, 2010, 2012) dismiss inclusive education as a political bandwagon. We reject these dismissals of inclusive education and reassertions of special education.

With respect to the notion of 'inclusion' in Africa, Phasha, Mahlo, and Dei (2017) suggest that: 'Inclusion is not a given in our communities' (p. 1). We would like to argue that it is. Ubuntu is a recognised theoretical ideology, which is evident in practice. It resonates with the humanistic spirit that clearly defines the ethos of the African peoples (Okeke, van Wyk, & Phasha, 2014; Berghs, 2017). It is a given in local communities, particularly in rural areas, by virtue of how they live and coexist. It is about:

- Valuing humanness – respect for human dignity; celebrate diversity, justice and fairness.
- Interdependence and dependence – Solidarity, collective co-operation, 'I am because you are'; it takes a village to raise a child, what is fair and just.
- Spirit of interconnectedness and social cohesion – social harmony; interpersonal relations; shared moral discourse; friendliness; consensus building, solidarity; open forms of communication.
- Spirit of compassion, hospitality and sharing – Deep caring; understanding of one another; supportiveness according to needs; sharing – material goods, knowledge, skills and human capital.

Africans have struggled for Ubuntu, a shared collective humanness and social ethics against oppression to maintain group cohesion (Berghs, 2017). It is this spirit that Kisanji (1998) suggests is what sets Africa apart from western ideals. He argues that customary education in rural Africa contradicts Western notions of inclusion and that customary education in in-tact rural communities of sub-Saharan Africa is characterised by elements of inclusion. This includes the provision of a relevant, locally developed 'curriculum' and the preparation of young people to become responsible citizens in their interdependent community structures. He pointed out that more recent attempts to formalise the process of inclusion, with the emphasis on 'special educational needs', have often ended in failure and the replication of traditional special educational tropes. Here he was talking about the inclusion of children with disabilities. We are inclined to agree with him from our encounters with teachers in Africa. Teacher trainees on short courses claimed that inclusion to them is about equality, equal opportunity, to be valued and respected, to belong, to be involved, to be given a fair chance. When asked what the local terms were which captured this concept, they suggested the following. These are just a few examples:

- Ubuntu (Nguni, South Africa)
- Akato Timihirt (Ethiopia)
- Ushirikishwaji (Swahili, Kenya)
- Kuba yincenye ngalokugcwele (Siswati, Swaziland).

Inclusion in Africa in a wider sense can be seen as a fight for freedom. Inclusion is never more necessary than in the African context, which has for many years been subjugated to oppression. Africa's fight for freedom stems from its history of colonisation and its continued struggle to achieve independence, mainly political and economic. According to Harper (2015), economic independence has proved to be beyond the grasp of African governments and so the struggle for complete independence has been difficult. Coupled with this is replacement of colonial power, not by democracy, but by variants of authoritarianism, leading to a general failure to improve living standards for the majority of people or real empowerment of ordinary citizens. To address these conditions, African countries continue to be reliant on external support. With this comes agendas for development, which may or may not be sustainable or appropriate for the African context. Freedom to find local solutions in Africa is difficult, but Njoroge (2004) argues this can be achieved with the development of social consciousness through education to enable Africans to pragmatically seek for solutions to national and continental problems (Njoroge, 2004). Berghs (2017) suggests that a shared collective humanness and social ethics against oppression epitomized by an 'Africa rising' discourse, to maintain group cohesion, otherwise known as Ubuntu in the African context, can facilitate this (Berghs, 2017).

When we look more closely at notions of 'inclusion' in the African context, we forward Chinedu Okeke and others' propositions as a way to begin thinking about inclusion in this continent. In the quest for freedom from discrimination and exclusion, as a continent, instead of looking elsewhere, they suggest that countries need to reflect on a set of Afrocentric theories, which are about africanisation, Ubuntu, and indigenous knowledge. African indigenous knowledge is about a lived world, a form of reasoning that informs and sustains people who make their homes in a local area, enabling people to get on with their lives in a particular geographical community. 'Too often, policy makers and technocrats are more influenced by global frameworks, than indigenous knowledge' (Kisanji & Saanane, 2009). These propositions may be applied to education for all, including those with disabilities.

Phasha, Mahlo, and Dei (2017) argue that this sense of inclusion within the African continent has to be struggled for and must evoke critical questions

'INCLUSION' IN THE AFRICAN CONTEXT

of power, equity and social difference. They assert that schooling in Africa needs to embrace difference while grappling with the teaching of indigeneity, decolonization and resistance. For Inclusive Education, this means the achievement of *sustainable* and appropriate education for *all* learners, including those with disabilities and special needs. We support these claims adding Njoroge's arguments on how this fight for inclusion can be part of the renaissance in Africa. Njoroge (2004) argues that to achieve liberation, creativity and social consciousness, which are inhibited by colonialism, neocolonialism and missionary work, are necessary in achieving the vision of renaissance in Africa. Njoroge argues that education is central to the development of social consciousness where learners are socialized into various moral and political values and that this requires Africans to pragmatically seek for solutions to national and continental problems.

In the following chapters, we examine the extent to which countries are seeking local solutions with respect to inclusion and inclusive education and how these are being translated into policy and practice.

4 Country Accounts

The fight for freedom, reconstruction and reparation in the face of conflict and struggles for independence, has resulted in consideration of more democratic inclusive policies in countries like Libya, Rwanda, Zanzibar, Ghana and South Africa.

Gadour's chapter on 'Challenging Inclusive Education Policy and Practice in Libya', provides a powerful account of how difficult it is to develop a more inclusive education system in a country in conflict. The conflicts have resulted in a number of challenging factors adversely influencing the provision of inclusive education both from a policy and a practice perspective. He argues that Libya where human rights are, in general, in crisis, inclusive education is necessary to bring positive social and political changes. He believes that this can be accomplished with a focused response from the Ministry of Education, which rests on empirical evidence for the factors affecting implementation of inclusive practice. Many children with special educational needs are allowed to attend regular classrooms in mainstream schools in Libya. However, they are highly unlikely to have their needs met within these classrooms owing to the lack of teachers' training within the area of special education. The key challenge is teacher attitudes. Teachers possess positive attitudes to inclusion but negative attitude towards inclusion of children with severe behavioural problems and mental illness within their classrooms. Gadour recognizes also the need to review assessment practices, which label and exclude children.

Karangwa's chapter entitled 'Strides and Strains in Including Children with Disabilities in Rwandan Education: Critical Reflections on Disability, Policies and Practice in Education Developments' is an encouraging account of Rwanda, a country which has risen from a traumatic past and responded positively to marginalization and exclusion. Karangwa presents a detailed account of the post-genocide reconstruction, which resulted in increased numbers of children accessing education. With the ever-increasing focus on school dropouts and increased access, these are not without challenges. Concerns are raised about the vicious cycle of disability, vulnerability and poverty within this context and persistent inadequacies in educational services for Children with Disabilities, and other basic rights. Cultural perceptions of disability and potential to participate in socio-economic developments, is a challenging feature in the planning process. Nevertheless, attention is given to the education of children with disabilities with the Special Needs Education Policy of 2007. The country's Vision 2020 strategy aims at achieving quality education for all learners by improving infrastructure and providing a range of social services.

Since the revolution in Zanzibar in 1964, developments included a renewed focus on education for all learners, including out of school children and dropouts. Juma provides interesting insight into this context in his chapter 'Towards Inclusive Education Development: Addressing the Gap between Rhetoric and Practice in Zanzibar Schools'. He highlights controversies around definitions around inclusive education in this context and use of excluding terminologies. He discusses the challenges around using English as a medium of instruction in the last two years, the tension between public vs private schooling, the lack of inclusive education in technical and vocational education, and the lack of teacher training.

Nketsia questions whether the Inclusive education policies and practices in Ghana are castles in the air or realizable post-independence in 1957 and the move towards educational access for all children. His chapter 'Inclusive Education Policy and Practice in Ghana: Air Castle or Realizable?' details the development of policy in Ghana. He highlights ambiguity and contradictions in conceptualisation of inclusion, which is regarded the same as integration, and the emphasis on screening, identification, diagnoses, referral and treatment of school children with disabilities. He described the move towards transforming special schools into resource centres as a positive move, although children remain segregated, for example children with severe and profound disabilities will remain in special schools and units. He describes the inclusive education pilot project, which had little impact on teachers' attitudes and school reform.

He also highlights positive government initiatives, which have addressed a range of barriers to school access, albeit schools remain unchanged in terms of curriculum, assessment and teaching and learning strategies to address the diversity of learning needs. Nketsia describes the implementation of Inclusive Education in Ghana as a 'castle in the air'; a dream which has not yet been fulfilled.

Naicker and Stofile's chapter on post-apartheid South Africa and the 'In Search of an Inclusive Pedagogy in South Africa' covers the challenges within the South Africa which point to the persistent rich-poor divide, poverty, crime, xenophobia and other forms of violence, which continue to marginalize and exclude learners. Naicker and Stofile highlight the difficulties in enabling inclusive pedagogy through the curriculum in light of the attention on performance. They discuss the impact on performance of children experiencing socio-economic conditions and trauma in the Western Cape province in South Africa. They argue that learners whose basic needs are not met are also not achieving success, despite the National School Nutrition programme in schools for learners from poor homes.

Kavua provides an insightful analysis of inclusive education and what this means in Kenya as integration, in his chapter 'In-Service Tutor Development in Support of Inclusive Education: Lessons From Partnerships Between University and Organisations'. Kenya's policy defined IE in its broadest sense as increasing the participation of all learners, but Kavua highlights some of the local resistance towards mainstreaming of children with disabilities. He presents an account of how the country responded post-independence from Britain in 1963 and the move towards integration for learners within specific categories of disability. He argues that the continuation of negative cultural beliefs on disability affects thinking and planning in this context. He highlights the challenges teachers face in implementing the policies, which relate to poor motivation, teachers' attitude towards learners with disabilities, rigid regular curriculum and inadequate trained teachers in inclusive education practices. One of the issues is that many schools do not possess the policies and remain unaware of expectations.

Lawrence presents an in-service tutor training initiative between Kyambogo University and Sightsavers in Uganda in his chapter 'Preparing In-service Tutor for Inclusion in Uganda through Partnerships between University and Development Partners'. Interestingly, colleges are including students with disabilities, but not from all categories. Classroom organization and improved accessibility are reported as positives. Gaps in professional training due to the lack of qualified staff in special education, is identified as a major challenge. Other challenges include a lack of funding, need for modification in functional assessment, adaptation of curriculum materials, development of alternative communication skills and modification of college environment, is noted. Lawrence highlights the need also for greater sensitization on the needs of students with disabilities and special educational needs.

Nxumalo's chapter 'Inclusive Education Policy Implementation in Swaziland: A Critical Reflection on Developments since 2011' details the history, rationale and framework of the Swaziland Education and Training Sector Policy (EDSEC), which incorporates an inclusive, cross-cutting approach to address the needs of a diversity of learners in this context. This policy is aligned to the Southern Africa Development Community (SADC) Framework and Programme of Action (2008–2015) for Comprehensive Care and Support for Orphans, Vulnerable Children, and Youth in SADC. A history of special needs in this context and the move towards inclusive education is detailed. Nxumalo discusses 'Inqaba' as a comprehensive inclusive school reform approach and Child Friendly Schools framework, employed in this context. Some of the challenges in this context point to the continued language associated with special education and deepseated discriminatory practices. Teacher training is identified as a key priority.

Side's chapter on the only country in Africa which has not been colonised, details the inclusive education policy in Ethiopia and the challenges regarding implementation. In 'Challenges of Implementing Inclusive Education and Supporting Marginalized Groups in Ethiopia', Side suggests that the key challenges are around the lack of a clear carrier structure relating to qualified special educators in the system to support implementation at each level. Capacity is lacking in terms of teacher training to support children with disabilities and special needs. This would include itinerant teachers placed at Resource Centres. Awareness of inclusive education as a concept is lacking with continued confusion with special needs and integration. Although efforts are being made to address this, implementation in practice is difficult due to the lack of knowledge and skills. Guidelines for curriculum differentiation and Individual education program were established in 2012 but these are not being followed in practice. Many students remain in schools without relevant assistive devices and physical accessibility in schools is an issue.

5 Summary

The chapters presented in this book support our claim that achieving inclusive education in Africa has not been without its challenges. However, what is encouraging is the development of legislative frameworks, which give impetus to realizing equal opportunities and social justice for all citizens. This is the starting point for the development of education policy reforms targeting all learners. There is clearly strong political will and this has emanated from the fight for freedom against colonization. Each country is unique in terms of its social and political histories, which have defined the way they have approached education for all. As we have argued before, inclusion for all within this continent is based on a fight for freedom from oppression and discrimination and this is evident from emerging legislation and policy. However, the question of whether this is being translated into practice is a question most authors in this book have attempted to address and the conclusion is a resounding no. Children who are out of school, dropped out and with disabilities remain at the periphery and are often the responsibility of charitable organisations working in the community, rather than the government. Barriers identified within each context relate to issues within and out of school – from negative parent and community attitudes, distance to school and lack of transport, lack of funding which includes corruption and embezzlement, to the lack of school infrastructure, physical accessibility, lack of resources and equipment, large class sizes, lack of inclusive pedagogy and assessment, lack of support personnel and restrictive medium of instruction.

When it comes to Inclusive Education as a part of the agenda for overall education reform, it is interesting to note how inclusive education has been defined either formally or informally. Many of the chapters discuss the conflation of inclusive education and integration and the focus primarily on special education and the enrolment of children with disabilities in mainstream settings. The lack of a consistent and clear definition of inclusive education within policy frameworks and teacher attitudes are identified as key barriers. In Juma's chapter on Zanzıbar, for example, although the policy includes a broad definition of inclusive education focusing on barriers within the system, the understanding on the ground remains fixated on barriers within the child. Attention is on children with disabilities rather than a host of other marginalizing factors which impact on learners' participation.

What is indeed heartening, is the way in which each author has engaged with the concept of inclusion as a way of understanding what inclusive education should look like in each country. They have engaged with international thinking and applied this to its significance in each context and how this can be enabled to bring about sustainable and appropriate change. Each provides a detailed analysis of their country's social and political history and how this has defined the agenda for educational reform. They recognize the rich diversity of cultures and communities within each country and the need to embrace all. They emphasise the need to focus and address the various barriers with the system and to focusing on *all* learners, particularly those experiencing barriers to learning and participation. Arguments presented are convincing as they are based on research within their contexts.

The authors are clearly passionate and committed to influencing change within their contexts and have provided some valuable recommendations for further policy development and support for teachers and schools. Generally, the focus, they argue, should be on improving the quality of education and provision of inclusive curricula, pedagogy and assessment to support achievement for all. The move should be away from a special education focus to greater inclusion for all. This is what makes this book important, to be read by thinkers, practitioners, including policymakers. The perspectives and arguments presented in this book are by local people. We have merely drawn from these and our experiences in Africa to present our own. These insights and arguments are offered as starting points for further debate and discussion, to move developments in Inclusive Education in Africa, forward.

References

Armstrong, F., Armstrong, D., & Barton, L. (Eds.). (2000). *Inclusive education: Policy, contexts and comparative perspectives*. London: David Fulton Publishers.

Barton, L., & Armstrong, F. (2007). *Policy, experience and change: Cross cultural reflections on inclusive education*. London: Springer.

Berghs, M. (2017). Practices and discources of ubuntu: Implications for an African model of disability. *African Journal of Disability, 6*, 2226–7220.

Booth, T., & Ainscow, M. (2016). *Index for inclusion: Guide to school development led by inclusive values*. Bristol: Centre for Studies in inclusive Education.

Boronski, T., & Hassan, N. (2015). *Sociology of education*. London: Sage Publications.

Brownell, M. T., & Smith, S. J. (2012). *Inclusive instruction: Evidence-based practices for teaching students with disabilities (what works for special-needs learners)*. New York, NY: The Guilford Press.

Clough, P., & Corbett, J. (2000). *Theories of inclusive education*. London: Paul Chapman Publishing.

Davis, P. (2003). *Including children with visual impairment in mainstream schools: A practical guide*. London: David Fulton Publishers Ltd.

Eide, A. H., Khupe, W., & Mannan, H. (2014). Development process in Africa: Poverty, politics and indigenous knowledge. *African Journal of Disability, 3*(2), 1–6.

Eleweke, C. J., & Rodda, M. (2002). The challenge of enhancing inclusive education in developing countries. *International Journal of Inclusive Education, 6*(2), 113–126.

Farrell, M. (2006). *Celebrating the special school*. London: David Fulton Publishers Ltd.

Farrell, M. (2010). *Debating special education*. London: Routledge.

Farrell, M. (2012). *New perspectives in special education: Contemporary philosophical debates.* & Abingdon: Routledge.

Fox, M. (2004). *Including children 3–11 with physical disabilities: Practical guidance for mainstream schools.* London: David Fulton Publishers Ltd.

Healy, J. M. (2011). *Different learners: Identifying, preventing, and treating your child's learning problems.* New York, NY: Simon & Schuster Paperbacks.

Kauffman, J. M., & Hallahan, D. P. (1995). *The illusion of full inclusion: A comprehensive critique of a current special education bandwagon.* Austin, TX: Pro-Ed.

Kauffman, J. M., & Sasso, G. (2006). Toward ending cultural and cognitive relativism in special education. *Exceptionality, 14*(2), 65–90.

Kisanji, J., & Saanane, C. B. (2009). *Responding to marginalization and exclusion in education in Tanzania.* Chapter prepared for the Research Forum, Institute for Inclusive Education, State University of Arizona, Arizona.

Mariga, L., McConkey, R., & Myezwa, H. (Eds.). (2014). s*Inclusive education in low-income countries. A resource book for teacher educators, parent trainers and community development.* Rondebosch: Disability Innovations Africa.

McConkey, R., & Bradely, A. (2010). Promoting inclusive education in low-income countries. In V. Timmons & P. N. Walsh (Eds.), *A long walk to school: Global perspectives in inclusive education.* Rotterdam, The Netherlands: Sense Publishers.

Mitchell, D. (2005). *Contextualizing inclusive education: Evaluating old and new international paradigms.* Oxfordshire: Routledge.

Muthukrishna, N. (Ed.). (2008). *Educating for social justice and inclusion in an African context pathways and transitions. New York, NY:* Nova Science Publishers Inc.

Njoroge, R. J. (2004). *Education for renaissance in Africa.* Canada: Trafford Publishing.

Nussbaum, M. C. (2011). *Creating capabilities: The human development approach.* Cambridge, MA: Harvard University Press.

Okeke, C., van Wyk, M., & Phasha, N. (2014). *Schooling, society and inclusive education.* Cape Town: Oxford University Press.

Oliver, M. (1990). *The politics of disablement.* London: Macmillan.

Oliver, M., & Barnes, C. (2012). *The new politics of disablement.* Basingstoke: Palgrave Macmillan.

Pather, S., & Nxumalo, C. (2012). Challenging understandings of inclusive education policy development in Southern Africa through comparative reflection. *International Journal of Inclusive Education, 17*(4), 420–434.

Perry, A. (2015). *The rift: A new Africa breaks free.* London: Weidenfield & Nicolson.

Phasha, N., Mahlo, D., & Sefa Dei, G. J. (Eds.). (2017). *Inclusive education in African contexts.* Rotterdam, The Netherlands: Sense Publishers.

Sen, A. (1999). *Development as freedom.* Oxford: Oxford University Press.

Slee, R. (2010). *The irregular school.* Abingdon: Routledge.

Slee, R. (2018). *Inclusive education isn't dead, it just smells funny.* Abingdon: Routledge.

Tomlinson, C. A. (2016). *The differentiated classroom: Responding to the needs of all learners (ASCD)*. Alexandria: ASCD.

UNESCO. (2015). *Education for all 2000 – 2015: Achievements & challenges*. Paris: UNESCO. Retrieved from http://unesdoc.unesco.org/images/0023/002322/232205e.pdf

UNESCO. (2016). *Education for people & planet: Creating sustainable futures for all. Global education monitoring report*. Paris: UNESCO. Retrieved from http://unesdoc.unesco.org/images/0024/002457/245752e.pdf

UNESCO. (2017). *A guide for ensuring inclusion and equity in education*. Paris: UNESCO. Retrieved from http://unesdoc.unesco.org/images/0024/002482/248254e.pdf

Waliaula, K. W. (2009). 'Negotiating local knowledge II: Kiswahili and attitudes toward disability'. *Disability Studies Quarterly, 29*(4), 5.

Whitehead, C. (2015). The contribution of the Christian missions to British colonial education. *International Journal of the History of Education, 35*(1), 321–337.

CHAPTER 1

Challenging Inclusive Education Policy and Practice in Libya

Abdelbasit Gadour

1 Introduction

It is fair to say that the area of inclusive education, particularly in the North African region, where the Arab Spring took place, has been a subject of concern, not only because of the lack of clear educational policies that inform practices within those countries, but also because of political, social and economic constraints. Indeed, these concerns are also integral to identifying the educational needs of children within mainstream schools and the contextual factors that bear down on, influence and restrict the practice of teachers in mainstream schools who are faced with the task of providing inclusive education.

Influenced by the recent revolutions that took place in the North African neighbouring countries, namely Tunisia and Egypt in 2010, the Libyans rose up and said enough is enough to 42 years of dictatorship. The 17th of February 2011 marked the Libyan Civil Uprising in the city of Benghazi against Muammar Gaddafi's regime, followed by unrest in all Libyan major cities. This led to the protesters capturing Gaddafi alive in his hometown Sirt on the 20th of October 2011. Two days later, the Libyans and the entire world witnessed the end of one tyrant's era, unaware that this one ending was to be a catalyst for the birth of many others, far worse. On the 23rd of October 2011, the leader of the National Transitional Council (NTC) announced that Libya was free and justice prevailed. It was widely hoped that the Civil Uprising in Libya would bring positive social and political changes and hence change the quality of education for all (Friedman, 2011). However, the legacy of Gaddafi's regime proved to be far more difficult to overcome than first anticipated; the dream for real democracy and social justice in Libya remain far from reaching a resolution as the struggle for power continues between all the parties concerned. As a result of this, Libya now has two governments; one of which is supported by the parliament in the east and the other, which is supported by the parliament in the west. A conflict of interest between the two authorities has continued, leaving the country on the edge of a split. Indeed, the current living standards and quality of life in Libya is far worse than during the old regime. The reasons behind this

© KONINKLIJKE BRILL NV, LEIDEN, 2019 | DOI:10.1163/9789004391505_002

are extremely complex and lie beyond the scope of this study. My intention in this chapter is to focus on the development of inclusive education within the educational system in Libya and the aim of this is to encourage positive social, political and economic changes. To do so, in the next section I shall explore some of the important literature that deals with the idea of inclusive educational practices.

2 Education from Historical Perspective

The location of Libya in relation to Africa, and Libya's fortunate geographical situation has made it a very attractive place for invaders from all over the world (e.g. Turks and Italians). Consequently, education in Libya developed under the influence, and to serve the needs, of its invaders, rather than that of the Libyan people. This continued across the whole of four centuries (1551–1951) (El-Fathaly et al., 1980; Deeb & Deeb, 1982; The National Report for Development of Education, 2008). Over the centuries, the Libyans were exposed to alien languages, cultures, history, ideologies and various forms of government legislations that made the Libyans second citizens. In fact, the Libyan children were educationally disadvantaged and marginalised, particularly during the period of the Italian colonisation to Libya (1911–1943), reflecting generations of total poverty and ignorance which still have an impact on the current educational system. The Italians controlled the education system and as such access to schools was limited to the Italians and to those Libyans who co-operated with them; it should be also noted that the curricula and medium of instruction in those schools were Italian. This was declared in the policy of the colonial administration which intended to limit the number of Libyan children beyond the primary level. In consequence, this forced those Libyans who wanted to have further education to travel abroad, particularly to Egypt or Tunisia, in order for them to continue their study in Arabic; this, however, was only available to those whose families were economically able to afford to do so.

Moreover, other forms of schooling had to be created by the Libyans to preserve their beliefs, traditions, Arabic language and Islamic education. This was mainly available in Islamic centres and mosques. Learning the Quran was a priority which involved mastering the Arabic language and, most importantly, discovering the principles of Islam. Indeed, the Libyan people saw education in religious moral terms and parents were expected to contribute to the teaching of their children as a principal duty of their religion. This reflects the idea that education was a shared responsibility between the "Kuttabs" or "Zawiyas" (centres of learning Quran and worship), where children are taught by the

Imams (Islamic teachers), and parents, whose duty in the evening was to listen to what their children had memorised from the Quran during the day. In these centres learning was free and everyone was welcome to attend, regardless of their age or background. Imams were working as volunteers, devoting their time to the well-being of the community, though on some occasions they might accept money, food and gifts – especially from those whose parents were well off. In general, Imams have always been respected and highly thought of as holy men and as a source of enlightenment and, as such, their quality of teaching, skills, knowledge and authority are indispensable. Children were very often reminded by their parents to behave and respect their Imams. Although this may suggest a mutual understanding based on religious principles between home and schools (Kuttabs), this should not imply that parents were always happy with the level of education and support available for their children (see Al-Shapani, 1996). In fact, the level of illiteracy prevalent amongst parents in those days made it almost impossible for them to get fully involved in the education of their children (Gadour, 2003). In addition, it was not always possible for young children to attend those centres due to their responsibilities towards their families, hardship and severe economic conditions. Indeed, families had great expectations that their children would provide additional labour on the family farm and help with animal herding and this was seen as a greater priority than their education. The lack of availability of schools and centres of teaching within walking distance was also another factor preventing many young children, particularly girls, from pursuing their education; for girls, leaving the family home in the early morning to walk a long distance was not an option, both in terms of their own protection and due to cultural restrictions.

After the defeat of the Italians in the Second War, Libya came under the administration of the superpowers of the time, namely the British, American and the French. A few primary and secondary schools were opened, representing two different educational systems. The British Palestinian educational system was introduced to the people of the provinces of Barqha and Tripoli, where the British had established supremacy over them, while France enforced the French Tunisian educational system in the province of Fezzan. Although this was perceived as an attempt by the colonial administration to divide the country and alter its inherited Islamic educational system, it did not weaken the national consciousness and solidarity of the Libyan citizens. The struggle for unity and independence against the new domination continued and included the aim to develop a more inclusive education system preserving the Libyan identity, language and culture (Fathaly, 1982). Yet, it should be highlighted that during the British and American administration, the Libyans held on to a sliver of hope that reform to the policy of education was possible within the national

Arab system. By the time of independence in 1951, young men were encouraged to seek knowledge from the most prominent places in the Arab world "ZaitunaMosque in Tunisia" and "El-Azhar University in Egypt".

3 Education Post-Independence

On the 24th of December 1951, Libya got its independence through the United Nation after months of negotiations. At the time, Libya was considered one of the poorest countries in the world with only ten percent of the population having been to school (Minister of Education, 1974). Although new autonomy sparked national interest in education within which free and compulsory primary education was advocated, the development of education policy at that time was very slow. It was a sense of their weakness and ignorance that encouraged the Libyan people to strive for the development of their education system. While some people donated their effort and time, others saw their wealth as a means of contributing to the effort and invested in converting buildings to schools. This should not in any way undermine the initiatives of the government to improve education in Libya. In fact, the concern for education was highlighted in three articles in the first Libyan constitution. These are still considered the milestones of the modern system of education in Libya:

> Article 28: Every Libyan shall have the right to education. The state shall ensure the diffusion of education by means of the establishment of public schools and of private schools which may permit to be established to under its supervision, for Libyans and foreigners.

> Article 29: teaching shall be unrestricted so long as does not constitute a breach of public order and it is not contrary to morality. Public education shall be regulated by law.

> Article 30: Elementary education shall be compulsory for Libyan children of both sexes; elementary and primary education in the public school shall be free. (Quoted in Deed & Deed, 1982, p. 28)

Indeed, from the time of independence onwards enormous efforts were made to develop a more inclusive education system, and so new schools were built and teachers were trained to acquire the necessary skills for teaching (Ministry of Education, 1974). The Libyan Government directly adopted the Egyptian educational system as a model that suited their own culture, and subsequently education became more accessible and free to everyone. Although the government found it difficult to achieve its targets in the first decade (the 1950s) owing to economic problems and the shortage of professionals, it managed to open the first university in Benghazi in 1955, and students were encouraged to continue their studies in higher education by offering them a small monthly allowance. In addition, religious education was given special consideration during the independence period with the extension of the Zawies centres into religious institutes with primary, preparatory and secondary levels for those who wish to continue their religious education. Also, an Islamic university was opened in the city of Al Beda, which featured religious and Islamic law faculties to teach Libyan students from religious institutes as well as students from all over the world.

As progress was made in the Libyan economy fuelled by the petroleum revenues during the 1960s, the country witnessed a rapid increase in the number of those who were enrolled in primary, intermediate, and secondary schools. By that time education was reaching quite a large number of the young Libyans. At primary level, the number of pupils in reached 270,617 pupils in 1968, compared with 65,164 in 1955; while at the intermediate level, the figure was 29,181 students in 1968 in comparison with only 2,585 in 1955 (Ministry of Education, 1974). Moreover, the number of primary schools had almost trebled: 1,069 schools in 1968, against only 376 schools in 1955. In contrast, the number of intermediate schools in 1955 had not been much increased in 1968 (8–25 respectively). Although the difference in number between the primary and secondary schools is noticeable, it might have been considered unwise to establish secondary schools on a wider scale until primary education had been firmly established. Furthermore, this quantitative growth also impacted on the number of teachers. In 1955, the numbers of teachers in primary, intermediate, and secondary schools was 2,061, 152, and 130 respectively; this is in contrast with 9,161, 2,076, and 608, respectively by 1968 (Ministry of Education, 1974; The National Report for Development of Education, 2008). More recently, as evidence of the progress towards inclusive education, the number of children enrolled at the basic education level (a combination of primary and intermediate education for children aged between 6–15) has reached 100% and this has now become a compulsory stage of education for all children throughout Libya (The National Report for Development of Education, 2008).

In spite of these developments, the educational system remains focussed on producing a large number of young people more qualified for administrative work rather than vocational employment. It also remains focussed on quantity rather than quality, and concentrates more on academic principles, as opposed to offering a more practical education (El-Fathaly et al., 1980; The National Report for Development of Education, 2008). There has also been growing concern with the rapid increase in the number of students enrolling into Libyan schools, especially given the shortages of school professionals in the field of special education and inclusion (Al-Shapani, 1996; The National Educational Report, 2000). In response to these acute shortages, teachers are under pressure to deal with large groups of students, across a wide ability range, entirely on their own. Al-Shapani has also noticed that the number of learners at all levels of education who may be vulnerable or at risk of exclusion or underachievement is still very high. This appears to be recurrent problem right up to the present day, which schools' professionals could not readily overcome (El-Fathaly & Palmer, 1980; Al-Shapani, 1996; The National Report for Development of Education, 2008). The UNESCO Report (2005) highlighted similar concern with regard to the increasing number of children excluded from quality education and who then consequently dropped out of the system. More recently The UNICEF Report (2013) has revealed similar concerns with regard to the increasing proportion of children unable to continue their education owing to the ongoing armed conflicts in Libya. Whilst this should not ignore the efforts made by the Libyan government over the years to develop a more inclusive education system, it is widely accepted that there is still a long way to go to establish a professional standard that can adequately respond to the educational needs of all Libyan children (UNICEF, 2013). In contrast with other countries in the region, there has been a dramatic change in the educational system in Libya, particularly in terms of quantity, with the number of schools, teachers and students increasing greatly. However, many classrooms in mainstream schools remain substandard, lacking effective teaching methods that encourage social communication skills and interaction between learners which seek to support understanding and acceptance between individual differences (Gadour, 2006; The World Bank, 2008; Arab Knowledge Report, 2009). The later report has also highlighted the important role of teachers in enhancing inclusive education through their practices. In line with teachers' practices I shall review the literature concerning the area of inclusive education and inclusion in Libya and draw some conclusions in contrast with previous research findings.

4   Inclusive Education

Although several studies have dealt with the historical development of the educational system in Libya, very little attention has been given to inclusive education and inclusion in general (The National Report for Development of Education, 2008). In searching the Libyan literature on inclusive education and inclusion policies, little has been found informed by research and experts in the field of education and consequently difficult to measure for credibility. In fact, inclusive education is a rather bewildering recent phenomenon in the education system in Libya. The international literature suggests that the concept of inclusive education is elusive and has different meanings in different contexts (Florian, 1998; Kavale & Forness, 2000; Dyson, 2003; Hodkinson, 2005; Singal, 2006; Friend & Bursuck, 2011). In other words, inclusive education is not a fixed concept, but a social construct that is dependent on the context and the needs to be addressed in that context (Darling-Hammond & Bransford, 2005). This is reflected in the various discrepancies among Libyan educators concerning the meaning of special education, inclusive education and inclusion. Whilst this could be attributed to the lack of a clear framework both for defining such terms and for clearly articulating Libyan educational strategy and policy, there is a common belief within schools and amongst teachers that children with special educational needs should be allowed to attend mainstream schools. This carries the proviso, the work of teachers and the work within the classroom is not disrupted. In other words, children with special educational needs are often left to their own devices, either to sink or swim. As a result of this, a great percentage of parents in Libya doubt the role of schools as social institutions that promote knowledge, personal and social skills, equality and enhance the well-being of all children (Gadour, 2003).

The UNICEF Report (2013) underlined the growing concern around significant shortages of school professionals specialising in the area of special education and psychological support; a gap which needs urgent attention in light of the psychological stress many children have experienced during the arm conflicts in Libya. In line with such concern, El-Shapani (1996) pointed out the general decline in the social behaviour and standards of learning among children in mainstream schools and suggested that unless these issues are effectively addressed by the educational authorities, the new generation of Libyans are at risk. The UNICEF Report has also highlighted the need to respond adequately to children's special educational needs within the mainstream schools, and described the current teachers' situation in Libya as in real crisis. It underlines areas such as teachers' income, training programmes and suggests that further courses on special education and inclusion must be reconsidered if teachers are to realise their full potential and for real inclusive education to happen. Equally, teachers should be reflecting upon their own approaches/methods of teaching and encouraging all children to participate in work-related activities, rather than relying on the old static formula of teaching (Gadour, 2007). In like manner, children should be encouraged to be independent and to be critical of any deficiency within the school system. There is also an urgent need to address the predominant methods of assessment within the mainstream school system, especially at the basic education level, where ability or success is measured merely by rather crude forms of examination. Year after year, this form of assessment has proved to be responsible for holding young children back from progressing with their counterparts (Gadour, 2007). Indeed, this form of assessment has led to a superficial approach to learning, which is largely responsible for children's failure to transfer what they have learnt in school to the real life outside the school. In fact, this approach has led to increasing academic failure and subsequently to exclusion from school (Gadour, 2007; The National Report for Development of Education, 2008).

UNESCO (1994) defined inclusive education in their Section for Special Needs Education which states that:

> The main point of inclusive education is the idea of every student learning together at any possible time notwithstanding the learning differences among them. The educational institutions practicing inclusive education should understand and respond to the various requirements of their students, being compliant to divers methods and rates of learning and making available quality education for every student by designing an effective curricula, organisational management, teaching skills, quality recourse use and corporation with the communities.

This suggests that schools and teachers need to recognise that all children develop differently and have different learning needs and, as such, they require to develop a mechanism where education and teaching methods are structured to address children's specific learning needs within mainstream schools. In general, most teachers in Libya have positive attitudes toward inclusive education (Gadour, 2006), however, they more often than not express concerns with regard to the implementation of an inclusive approach, reflecting a great deal of day to day classroom teaching pressure and lack of resources (Gadour, 2006; Dybdahl & Ryan, 2009; Idol, 2006). Indeed, using an inclusive approach requires teachers to use teaching strategies and methods to make the curricula accessible and beneficial to all learners (Frattura & Capper, 2006; Idol, 2006; McLeskey & Waldron, 2007; Stanford & Reeves, 2009). The aim of this is to provide all children with every opportunity to successful learning experience and quality education (Miles & Singal, 2010).

The relevance of this chapter to current educational practice in the Arab world is supported by insights from previous published research I have carried out in Libya (Gadour, 2006, 2007). It is interesting to note from these research findings that teachers had positive perceptions on inclusive education in general; however, they appeared to have negative attitudes towards inclusion of children with severe behavioural problems and mental disabilities within their classrooms. Teachers attributed these negative perceptions to their lack of training in special needs education and to the lack of resources available for them in schools. Hence, a great number of children with special educational needs in Libya, especially boys, are segregated from other pupils in addition to being referred to professionals e.g. social workers and educational psychologists (EPs). A similar gender ratio, which points to the particular vulnerability of boys, is also found in other research of the assessment of pupils with special educational needs (Armstrong et al., 1993). Consequently, in Libya many of them abandon their mainstream schools for technical and vocational institutions. School teachers still blame children's emotional and behavioural difficulties on family factors (for example, illiterate parents and poor dynamics of relationships within the family (Gadour, 2006), even though the majority of the children were ostensibly referred because of learning difficulties and lack of concentration. While this may reflect the lack of inclusive practices with the educational system, it also underlines the conflict between parents and school professionals in which each party attributes children's problems to factors beyond their control (Armstrong, 1995; Gadour, 2006; Wheldall & Merrett, 1988). It is also important to highlight the fact that teachers in mainstream schools in Libya, like elsewhere, still spend considerable time on their own, trying to manage difficult behaviour in order to maintain classroom control. In like manner, mainstream school teachers find it extremely difficult to deal with low intelligence children or those who suffer from neurological or psychological disturbance, or those with severe behaviour problems (Libyan National Report for Development of Education, 2008). The Libyan National Report for Development of Education has also highlighted deficiencies within mainstream schools in meeting the needs of children experiencing such difficulties and, consequently, children are still excluded from schools and referred to special centres to pursue their education. Hence, nothing seems to have changed post the 2011 revolution in Libya. Teachers feel that managing difficult behaviour in classroom is a major concern which presents significant challenges to them as well as preventing inclusive education to take place.

In a previous study concerning the rhetoric of inclusive education in Libya, an attempt was made to understand the obstacles to special educational provisions within mainstream schools in Libya (Gadour, 2007); in another study, children were empowered to voice their opinion in relation to their learning and emotional and behavioural difficulties (Gadour, 2006); the opinions and views of teachers were also sought to understand and clarify what support was available for them to respond to children's difficulties within mainstream schools (Gadour, 2003). All of this was aimed at improving educational practices and informing policymakers around the issue of inclusive education in Libya. It is rather unfortunate to note that children's rights remain in crisis in Libya and nothing has changed post the 2011 revolution (UNICEF Report, 2013), although the educational system continues to allow children with various special educational needs to receive their education together with their age appropriate peers in regular classrooms within mainstream schools. Yet it is not widely appreciated that inclusion is about more than the simple place where children are educated – in mainstream or special school – or that the concerns around education for all seem to reflect an understanding of the benefits of an inclusive approach in the wider society. In the absence of a clear framework to identify the educational needs of children within mainstream schools in Libya, the struggle to appreciate those needs and what inclusive education is really about continues. Lawson (2005) suggested that inclusive education is about the involvement of all learners in conventional learning environments, where the participation of all learners allows optimum levels of attainability. Others view inclusive education as a method of achieving human rights in social relationships and creating a consensual, participatory ethos that enables all learners to take part in the curriculum and minimises any form of marginalisation (Booth, 1999; Clough & Corbett, 2000). The Department of Education (2005) described inclusive education as a simultaneous response to meet the needs of children of different backgrounds and different abilities within their mainstream schools. In doing so, inclusive education is seen as a way of building an inclusive community and an academic system that allows all learners to participate and progress academically, emotionally and socially (Landsberg & Kruger, 2005). Drawing on the present situation in Libya, where human rights are, in general, in crisis, inclusive education is badly required to bring positive social and political changes through investment in human development. This may suggest that all the stakeholders and decision makers in Libya need to review current educational practices within the mainstream school system and rethink educational policies. This is aimed at supporting the rights of children to have equal access to quality education and understanding how that can influence their lives and that of the many others around them. In line with this approach, Allan (2006) stated that inclusion should be concerned with schools and professionals as well as with the educational needs of children. While Barton (1997) holds the opinion that to achieve education for all, schools need to change their cultures and practices, and as such he believes inclusive education is not about:

> "special" teachers meeting the needs of "special" children in ordinary schools ... It is not merely about placing disabled pupils in classrooms with their non-disabled peers; it is not about "dumping" pupils into an unchanged system of provision and practice. Rather, it is about how, where and why, and with what consequences, we educate all pupils. (Barton, 1997, p. 234)

This says a lot about the way we think and conduct our lives, the philosophy that sustains each of us and the society in which we live; and centrally, about the empowerment of education. It could be argued that inclusive education in a society such as Libya is a myth reflecting decades of disempowerment, subordination and arbitrary forms of educational assessment (Gadour, 2006), all of which have influenced the rights of children and teachers alike, in one way or another. Certainly, the late call for inclusive education and inclusion depicted in The National Report for Development of Education (2008) has not been supported by the present political conflicts in Libya. In a similar way, the educational policies and legislation have been fuelled by the difference in views and opinions among decision makers and stakeholders in education, due to the existence of dual government system in Libya reflecting a fragmented society. It is rather sad to note that the present conflict of interests between the various authorities in Libya has not only affected the political and economic situation, but also the educational system as a whole, exposing children and teachers to unnecessary pressure and further challenges. It goes without saying that the post 2011 revolution era in Libya has not only been a challenging time for children with special educational needs, but also for teachers and schools to ensure inclusive educational practices. Although teachers may appear to support inclusive education, in practice they are reluctant to include children with severe behaviour problems and other mental disabilities in their classrooms (see Gadour, 2007), reflecting the lack of school resources and inadequate training in the field of special education. In line with this, the teachers' union in Libya has recently announced a national strike demanding extra support, incentives, resources, training, and equal rights compared with other professionals (e.g. doctors, judges, etc.) This strike continued for four weeks causing harmful damage to the education of all children and their well-being (see Libya-al-mostakbal.org, 2017). Thus, to implement positive changes within the educational system and encourage inclusive education in Libya, teachers must be involved and consulted by the educational authorities concerning educational policies, curriculum design and method of assessments.

5 Conclusion

I certainly found writing about inclusive education in Libya a challenging task. This is not only because of the lack of information and research in Libya concerning inclusive education, but also because of the wider implications of the notion which is used interchangeably by educators all over the world. In this chapter, I have made an attempt to review the literature dealing with the development of the education system in Libya. I have done this to articulate my understanding of the development of inclusive education in the Libyan context. There is a general belief that inclusive education arises from a notion of inclusion that is of paramount importance; that is, that all human beings are equal and as such they should be given equal opportunity. Inclusive education is considered essential for creating a comprehensive society; it is seen as the main vehicle for achieving social, political and economic development (Abi-Mershed, 2010; El Amine, 2005). In Libya, despite enormous efforts to enable young children to have access to education since independence in 1951, which resulted in the percentage of children entering the education system at its basic level reaching a 100% in 2008 (The National Report for Development of Education, 2008), there still remains a problem in achieving social objectives and meaningful education for all children. It is well noted that although many children with special educational needs are allowed to attend regular classrooms in mainstream schools in Libya, they are highly unlikely to have their needs met within these classrooms owing to the lack of teachers' training within the area of special education. This issue has been highlighted in a number of national educational reports (For example, The National Report for Development of Education, 2008). This underlines the fundamental role that teachers play in developing an inclusive education. Certainly, the question is no longer should children with special educational needs be included in mainstream classrooms or not, but how can inclusion be sustained, improved and made more effective for all children? Indeed, there is an urgent need to support inclusive education at the basic educational level through introducing more flexible framework of assessment, teaching methods/strategies and curriculum designed with inclusion in mind. The focus of education should not be on academic success alone, but should also should include children's personal and social development.

Unfortunately, children are still categorised, segregated and excluded at the basic educational level due to lack of successful strategies, methods/approaches of instruction, all of which are influenced by rather rigid framework of assessment (see Gadour, 2007). There is certainly a need to move away from an assessment led education system at the basic education level to more inclusive education, allowing vulnerable children to learn, progress and be regularly assessed in classrooms without constant fear and concern about passing or failing the end of year exams. It is concerning to see, in practice, at a basic educational level, children as young as nine and ten years old, being held back as a result of failing end of year exams. This implies that a student repeating the year would study the same subjects/modules once more, often with the same teachers and sadly with younger age group of children. This too often proves to be a debilitating experience for children, and one that all too often leads to them dropping out, or being excluded from mainstream schools (for more details on this, see Gadour, 2006, 2007).

Therefore, for inclusive education to happen effectively in mainstream schools in Libya, we need to review the framework of assessment and explore the reasons behind children's academic failure. Schools and teachers may need to adjust the curriculum in accordance with learners' differences. In a similar way, there is a need to examine the roles and responsibilities of teachers and schools in relation to the barriers to inclusive educational practices. The aim of this is to outline and articulate a clear rationale and, from this, to develop a strategic vision that addresses the problem of exclusion within mainstream schools in Libya. There is also a need for educational reform in Libya to provide quality education for all learners to prepare them for the demands of a postmodern technological world (see 2011 TIMSS results, www.timss.bc.edu; Arab Knowledge Report, 2009). We need to trigger positive changes in schools at classroom level, particularly in improving inclusive classroom practices, and also by improving the ethos of our schools. This will help to develop and support our young people and lead to an improvement in the students' achievements (Faour, 2012; The last World Bank Middle East and North Africa (MENA) development report, The World Bank, 2008).

In this chapter, a light has been shone on the impact of the ongoing armed conflicts and other emergencies in Libya, and the way in which these have compounded a number of challenging factors, which adversely influence the provision of inclusive education at the basic education level. Indeed, a greater awareness of the significance of inclusive education is needed, not only to improve the current educational practices in mainstream schools, but also for a more inclusive, coherence and stable society. At present, Libya face tough challenges and it is on the edge of civil war storming across the entire country. In these circumstances, inclusive education is in greater demand than ever to bring positive social, political and economic changes. It is hoped that the discussion in this chapter will help all stakeholders in Libya – the present educational authorities, the Ministry of Education, teachers and mainstream schools – and encourage them to argue for, and to support, quality education for all children. Perhaps now is the time to move away from a model that focusses on quantitative outcomes and begins to seriously prioritise qualitative goals.

It is a model that sees education as being child centred, and values the overall development of each individual student. Further empirical research is certainly needed to further understand the challenging factors that are restricting the implementation of more effective inclusive education practices within mainstream schools in Libya.

References

Abi-Mershed, O. (2010). The politics of Arab educational reform. In O. Abi-Mershed (Ed.), *Trajectories of education in the Arab world: Legacies and challenges* (pp. 1–12). New York, NY: Routledge advances in Middle East and Islamic Studies.

Allan, J. (2006). The repetition of exclusion. *International Journal of Inclusive Education, 10*(2–3), 121–133.

Al-Shapani, O. (1996). *The problems that face education in Libya and ways of overcoming them.* Tripoli: Tripoli Press.

Arab Knowledge Report. (2009). *Towards productive intercommunication for knowledge* (Produced by Mohammed bin Rashid Al Maktoum Foundation (MBRF) and the United Nation Development Programme/Regional Bureau for Arab States (UNDP/RDAS)). Dubai: Al Ghurair Printing and Publishing House LLC.

Armstrong, D. (1993). The assessment of special educational needs and the proletariatisation of professionals. *British Journal of Sociology of Education, 14*(4), 399–408.

Armstrong, D. (1995). *Power and partnership in education: Parents, children and special education.* London: Routledge.

Barton, L. (1997). Inclusive education: Romantic, subversive or realistic? *International Journal of Inclusive Education, 1*(3), 231–242.

Booth, T. (1999). Viewing inclusion from a distance: Gaining perspective from comparative study. *Support for Learning, 14*(4), 164–168.

Clough, P., & Corbett, J. (2000). *Theories of inclusive education: A student's guide.* London: Sage Publications.

Darling-Hammond, L., & Bransford, J. (2005). *Preparing teachers for a changing world: Report of the committee on teacher education of the national academy of education.* San Francisco, CA: Jossey-Bass.

Department of Education. (2005). *Conceptual and operational guidelines for the implementation of inclusive education: District-based support teams.* Pretoria: Department of Education.

Deeb, M., & Deeb, J. (1982). *Libya since the revolution: Aspect of social and political development.* New York, NY: Praeger.

Dybdahl, C. S., & Ryan, S. (2009). Inclusion for students with fetal alcohol syndrome: Classroom teachers talk about practice. *Preventing School Failure, 53*(3), 185–196.

Dyson, A. (2003). The Gulliford lecture: Special needs in the twenty: First century: Where we've been and where we're going. *British Journal of Special Education, 28*(1), 24–29.

El Amine, A. (2005). Executive summary. In A. El Amine (Ed.), *Reform of general education in the Arab world* (pp. 321–368). Beirut: UNESCO.

El-Fathaly, O. I. (1980). *Political development and social change in Libya*. Lexington, MA: Lexington Books.

Faour, M. (2012). *The Arab world's education report card: School climate and citizenship skills*. Washington, DC: The Carnegie Middle East Center. Retrieved October 3, 2017, from http://carnegieendowment. org/files/school_climate.pdf

Farrell, P. (1995). *Children with emotional and behavioural difficulties: Strategies for assessment and intervention*. London: The Falmer Press.

Florian, L. (1998). An examination of the practical problems associated with the implementation of inclusive education policies. *Support for Learning, 13*(3), 105–108.

Florian, L. (1998). Inclusive practice: What, why and how. In C. Tilstone, L. Florian, & R. Rose (Eds.), *Promoting inclusive practice* (pp. 13–26). London: Routledge.

Frattura, E., & Capper, C. (2006). Segregated programs versus integrated comprehensive service delivery for all learners. *Remedial and Special Education, 27*(6), 355.

Friedman, G. (2011). Libya, the west and the narrative of democracy. *Afgazad, 21*, 6–11.

Friend, M., & Bursuck, W. (2011). *Including students with special needs: A practical guide for classroom teachers*. Upper Saddle River, NJ: Prentice-Hall.

Gadour, A. (2003). *An investigation into perspectives on children experiencing emotional and behavioural difficulties with special reference to the Libyan context* (Unpublished thesis). University of Sheffield, Sheffield.

Gadour, A. (2006). Libyan children's views on the importance of school factors which contributed to their emotional and behavioural difficulties. *Journal of School Psychology International, 27*(2), 171–191.

Gadour, A. (2007). The rhetoric of inclusive education education in Libya: Are children's rights in crisis? In L. Barton & F. Armstrong (Eds.), *Policy, experince and change: Cross-cultural reflections on inclusive education*. Dordrecht: Springer.

Hodkinson, A. (2005). Conceptions and misconceptions of inclusive education: A critical examination of final-year teacher trainees' knowledge and understanding of inclusion. *Research in Education, 73*(1), 15–28.

Idol, L. (2006). Toward inclusion of special education students in general education. *Remedial and Special Education, 27*(2), 77.

Kavale, K. A., & Forness, S. R. (2000). History, rhetoric, and reality analysis of the inclusion debate. *Remedial and Special Education, 21*(5), 279–296.

Landsberg, E., Kruger, D., & Nel, N. (2005). *Addressing barriers to learning: A South African perspective*. Pretoria: Van Schaik.

Lawson, H. (2005, August 1–4). *Understandings of inclusion: The perceptions of teachers and teaching assistants*. Paper presented at Inclusive and Supportive

Education Congress (ISEC), International Special Education Conference, Inclusion: Celebrating Diversity? Glasgow, Scotland.

Libya-al-mostakbal.org. (2017). *Libya AL Mostakbal* [online]. Retrieved October 5, 2017, from http://www.libya-al-mostakbal.org

McLeskey, J., & Waldron, N. (2007). Making differences ordinary in inclusive classrooms. *Intervention in School and Clinic, 42*(3), 162.

Ministry of Education. (1974). *Development of education in the Libyan Arab Republic from the Othman Rule to the Present time.* Tripoli: Ministry of Education Publications.

Singal, N. (2006). Inclusive education in India: International concept, national interpretation. *International Journal of Disability, Development and Education, 53*(3), 351–369.

Stanford, B., & Reeves, S. (2009). Making it happen: Using differentiated instruction, retrofit framework and universal design for learning. *Teaching Exceptional Children Plus, 5*(6), 4.

UNESCO. (1994). *The Salamanca statement and framework on special education.* Paris: UNESCO.

UNESCO. (2003). *Overcoming exclusion through inclusive approaches in education: A challenge and a vision.* Paris: UNESCO.

UNESCO. (2005). *Guidelines for inclusion: Ensuring access to education for all.* Paris: UNESCO.

UNICEF Annual Report. (2013). *Libya.*

The National Report for Development of Education. (2008). *Libya.*

The United Nations Report. (1998). *Education in Libya.* Geneva: United Nations.

The World Bank. (2008). *MENA development report: The road not traveled: Education reform in the Middle East and North Africa.* Washington, DC: The World Bank.

The World Bank Group. (2012). *Launch of the Arab regional agenda for improving education quality.* Retrieved October 11, 2017, from http://web.worldbank.org/WBSITE/EXTERNAL/TOPICS/EXTEDUCATION/0,,contentMDK:23081869~menuPK:282428~pagePK:64020865~piPK:51164185~theSitePK:282386,00.html

Werhane, P. H., Hartman, L. P., Moberg, D., Englehardt, E., Pritchard, M., & Parmar, B. (2011). Social constructivism, mental models, and problems of obedience. *Journal of Business Ethics, 100*(1), 103–118.

Wheldall, K., & Merrett, F. (1988). Which classroom behaviour problems do primary school teachers say they find most troublesome? *Educational Review, 40*, 13–27.

CHAPTER 2

Strides and Strains in Including Children with Disabilities in Rwandan Education: Critical Reflections on Disability, Policies and Practice in Education Developments

Evariste Karangwa

1   Introduction

A close examination of a number of Rwandan policies, legislations and programs in the last two decades, reveal unambiguous Government's impetus in equalization of opportunities for all citizens, and a deliberately renewed attention to all marginalized groups that include those with disabilities (Republic of Rwanda, 2003a, 2007b, 2010a, 2011a, 2011b). The observation is equally shared by related studies in Rwanda (Williams, Abbott, & Mupenzi, 2015; Talley & Brintnell, 2016). Investigating the hidden causes of school dropout in Rwandan fee-free schooling programs for example, Williams et al. (2015) maintain that:

> Rwanda's legal framework characterises children's schooling as a fundamental right, one in which financial constraints should not be a basis for exclusion. The country's Constitution describes primary education as free and compulsory ... Subsequent policies articulated more specific approaches to address the situation of particular groups – for example, the Strategic Plan for Street Children of 2005, the Special Needs Education Policy of 2007, the Girls' Education Policy of 2008, and the Early Childhood Development Policy of 2011. (pp. 934–935)

This chapter points out that the conventional understanding of Rwanda's education policies are clearly focused on increasing access to basic schooling in disadvantaged communities and eliminating structural or material barriers to schooling (p. 935), however, hardly any attention is paid to factors that lead to school dropout and stagnation. In many ways, Maya Kalyanpur's (2008) reflective analysis of India's inclusive education policy and corresponding service provisions, appear to explain the Rwandan contexts:

© KONINKLIJKE BRILL NV, LEIDEN, 2019 | DOI:10.1163/9789004391505_003

> Can the government provide effective and sufficient schooling to all disadvantaged groups? Or, when resources are scant, do the goals of quantity and quality become mutually exclusive? Conversely, in trying to meet both goals, does it mean that neither is achieved? Not espousing inclusive education as a moral imperative would have alienated the international aid community and national disability rights activists, among others, jeopardizing India's position as a leader in the developing world. (pp. 256–257)

It is equally apparent therefore, that the declared Rwandan government promises to all disadvantaged groups seem to meet difficulties during their translations into corresponding services that include educational provisions for Children with Disabilities (CwD). Peculiarly, related studies and reflections in sub-Saharan African contexts seem to reveal closely comparable policies and practices in education of CwD (Christie, 2008; Filmer, 2008; Talley & Brintnell et al., 2016). Benefiting from studies in Nigeria and Zambia for example, Talley et al.'s (2016, p. 367) research on support services to inclusive education in Rwanda, acclaim numerous and easily accessible national policies and non-governmental organisation's (NGO) reports on education of CwD, and go on to express regret for the conspicuously absent information on the full scope of barriers to education as well as clearly mapped out solution proposals. They share the author's earlier views (Karangwa, Ghesquire, & Devlieger, 2007; Karangwa, Miles, & Lewis, 2010), underlining the persistence of attitudinal, cultural, physical and economic obstacles, and inadequately trained educators as the major setbacks to CwD's schooling. They suggest that the ongoing education reforms that deliberately stress support services for CwD's education are also likely to mark the way forward in finding sustainable solutions.

In essence, the controversy that seem to emerge from the government promises for education of CwD like other marginalized groups, and achievements made or difficulty met in the course of striving to meet policy missions and objectives, are the core subject of study in the present chapter.

2 Approach

The present chapter is a product of reflective investigations that takes advantage of the author's experiences in Rwandan inclusive education developments, especially his role in policy development for Rwandan Ministry of Education and related education institutions, as well as evaluation of inclusive and special Needs education projects and provisions in Rwandan communities and schools. The experiences have continually impelled his concerns, also

INCLUDING CHILDREN WITH DISABILITIES IN RWANDAN EDUCATION 33

expressed differently through various forums (Karangwa, 2003; Karangwa et al., 2007, 2010; Karangwa & McGeown, 2013; Handicap International, 2015). The present chapter thus, attempts to explore the developments in political strategies and programs, particularly investigating the extent to which these are made to address educational needs of CwD at the grassroots levels, through three major theoretical reviews:

1. National policies and related strategic instruments that specify the Rwandan government orientation and commitments to the education of CwD.
2. Studies conducted in Rwandan schools and communities in relation to education of CwD, as well as related reports and literature in the field.
3. Evaluation through the author's previous studies and extensive field experiences that include his involvement in policy developments and practice in Rwandan inclusive education.

The review approach through the three theoretical units intended to guide the investigation processes is the key factor to note, for it is geared towards a better understanding of the complex socio-political phenomena surrounding Rwandan CwD's education. The approach likens Cohen, Manion, and Morrison's (2003, p. 75) and Goetz and LeCompte's (1984, p. 68) ideas of analytic units prompting and guiding inquiry focus, approach and design. In this sense, the author's position as a Rwandan education professional is quite significant, for it also justifies self-reflective discourse on the nature, rationality and justifications of factors influencing Rwandan CwD's education. A position described by Guba and Lincoln (1994) and Mertens (2003) as epistemological, in light of which, the researcher's trustworthiness and ability as an inside translator of social and cultural trends (Denzin & Lincoln, 2000, p. 15) are key.

The investigation thus crisscrosses documented policy strategies, attempting to analyse the extent to which these are translated into appropriate practice. In the next sections, it looks into socio-political factors that influence school attendance for CwD, or significantly account for their dropout and/or stagnation rates in Rwandan schools. The inquiry will start by tracing the historical backdrop trends; will assess the current status, challenges and advances in Rwandan education for CwD; and basing on policy analyses and related studies, will strive to delineate explanations through the prevailing contexts of the country.

3   Background of Education for Children with Disabilities in Rwanda

Studies that had earlier addressed developments in education of Rwandan CwD, trace the slow progress in a three-staged evolutional pattern (Karangwa,

2014; Karangwa, Muhindakazi, & Iyamuremye, 2013) as explained in the next sections. In all stages however, the roles of charity, benevolence, community and political trends; emerge as the main features or key contributing agents in education of Rwandan CwD since 1960s.

3.1 *The Period of Benevolence and Charity*

The name of Father Josephe Fraipont Ndagijimana (1919–1982), a Belgian Priest of the White Fathers (Catholic order), continues to be an icon of compassion among Rwandan people with disabilities, for his benevolent services to children and youths with disabilities since 1960. According to Karangwa et al. (2013, p. 22), Home de la Vierge des Pauvre (HVP) was founded by the priest, and started educating the Deaf and the Blind youths by1962 in Nyanza sector of the Southern Province. The center for the Deaf was entrusted to Brothers of St Gabriel in Butare (in Huye District) in 1973, while the Brothers of Charity in Gatagara (in Nyanza District) were entrusted with education of children with Visual and physical impairments. Since then, HVP's charity and benevolence was the only source of support to educational and rehabilitation services for Rwandan CwD as reported by Karangwa (2014):

> One of the eminent historical reality is the fact that persistent marginalization of learners with Special Educational Needs (SEN), is also owed to the colonial governments (German & Belgian, 1894–1962) and even the post-colonial policies, both of which hardly accorded any considerations to the education of learners with disabilities ... founded in 1960, HVP received the first government support in 2010 in form of teachers' salaries and educational resources. (p. 48)

Accordingly, because of limited community support and political drive, the majority of CwD continued to go back to their villages after completing primary education without any professions, and HVP Gatagara center had to put in place vocational training programs by 1994. Until the devastations of the 1994 genocide against Tutsi that destroyed and halted most of the services, the centers initiated by Fr Fraipont in collaboration with Brothers of St Gabriel and of Charity respectively, remained the most prominent service providers for CwD's education.

3.2 *The Period of Open Door Policies*

The services of the Catholic Orders dominated the education of CwD most of the pre-genocide periods, and expanded with the post-genocide programmes (1994–2004), which was justifiably also the country's difficult reconstruction period. However, social reconciliation and cohesion programs during the period, also brought along renewed focus on disadvantaged groups, or the birth of advocacy lobby for genocide survivors, women, children, minority groups and the disabled, and are still featuring prominently (Byanafashe & Rutayisire, 2011; Karangwa et al., 2007; Republic of Rwanda, 2005). Groupe Scolaire (G.S) Gahini became the first ordinary and government-aided secondary school to open its doors for the visually impaired students in 1997 for example. An initiative expressed by the author as a *'bold and daring'* at the time (Karangwa, 2003), because it was not yet necessarily government-supported priority, rather a clear demonstration of attitude changes in some Rwandan communities, towards what is coined locally as *'Uburezi Budaheza'* or 'Non-exclusionary Education' (Karangwa, 2003; Karangwa et al., 2007). In fact, Talley et al.'s (2016) study actually reflects a place for CwD within the country's difficult socioeconomic reconstruction:

> ... the notion of educating children with disabilities (CwD) with their non-disabled peers in mainstream classrooms has only surfaced in African nations such as Rwanda more recently ... Rwanda, a small landlocked country in East Africa, has made tremendous strides in its education reform following the genocide in 1994 ... The progressive goals put forward in the government document' vision 2020 positions Rwanda to become a middle-income country by the year 2020. (p. 365)

It was not until 2000 when the Ministry of Local government (created in 1999) published its 'National Decentralization Policy', followed by the 'Community Development Policy' of 2002 and the 'Policy of Orphans and Vulnerable groups' of 2003 that CwD's needs were first apparent. However, despite the persistently unnoticeable support to CwD's education, Rwanda's commitment to education of the children was first legally articulated in the 2003 Constitution (Art. 40), Law N° 29/2003 of 30/08/2003 (Art. 2), and the 2003 Policies (Republic of Rwanda, 2003a, 2015a). The experience in G.S. Gahini (cited above) was a clear demonstration that the vulnerable children, for whom schools opened their doors at the time, increasingly included those with disabilities. The situation was actually confirmed by the rise in number of students with significant disabilities that pressed for registration in Rwandan Universities since 2001, and finally admitted in 2008 on an affirmative action program (Karangwa, 2008).

3.3 The Period of Policy Commitments to Inclusion

Though the Rwanda Government was signatory to earlier UN conventions (UNESCO Salamanca statement on Inclusive Education of 1994 and the

Convention on the Rights of a Child of 1989), its commitments to education of CwD was first articulated in the first post-genocide constitutional review of 2003 (Articles 28 and 40), which also called for related ministerial decrees and legislations (Republic of Rwanda, 2003a, 2007b, 2015a).

It is equally noted that law No. 01/2007 of 20th January 2007 that included rights to education of Rwandans with disabilities (Articles 11, 12 and 13) was ratified a year before the country signed (on 15th December 2008) the UN Convention on the Right of People with Disabilities (CRPD). However, it availed legal foundation for subsequent policy strategies and related instruments (Republic of Rwanda, 2007b, 2009b). Goal 1 for the current five year Education Sector Strategic Plan (ESSP 2013–2018) for example, pledges expansion of access to education at all levels of schooling for all children (Republic of Rwanda, 2013a, p. 38), including children with special needs (p. 43) by availing more disability-friendly facilities, training of teachers in related skills and by prioritizing special-needs-related measures.

Besides, the Nine Year-Basic Education (9YBE) program that worn the Common-Wealth-award on 29th August 2012 was declared by the Rwandan government in 2009 to accord free nine years of schooling to all disadvantaged children, and was subsequently upgraded to Twelve Years of Free education (12YBE) in 2012. HVP centers initiated by Fr Fraipont fifty years earlier for example, had developed into five centers by 2005, three of which were supported by the government and upgraded to both 9YBE and 12YBE (Karangwa, 2014) to respectively educate children with visual, hearing, physical and cognitive challenges.

As expounded in the next sections therefore, this period did not only mark renewed socio-political impetus and initiatives of all actors in Rwandan Education, but also challenges and expansion in schooling for all Rwandan children, including those with a wide range of disadvantages and disabilities (Republic of Rwanda, 2013a).

3.4 Developments in Education of Rwandan Children with Disability
The background of CwD's education in Rwanda discussed in the previous sections has prompted an exclusive probe into current developments, with particular focus on policy frameworks, opportunities or challenges in Rwandan education for school age children and youths with disabilities.

3.5 Policy and Legal Frameworks
It was stressed above that the first post-genocide constitution of 4th June 2003 was Rwanda's foundational milestone, for it articulated the country position in supporting marginalized groups (Republic of Rwanda, 2003a, 2015a).

Accordingly, Rwanda's legal framework characterises schooling as a fundamental right, emphasizing the need for empowerment of all girls and boys through education and training for their subsequent contribution to national development (Republic of Rwanda, 2008a, 2010a, 2012a, 2013a, 2013b). The country's approach to education is in fact stressed in the country's development strategic policy Vision 2020 (Republic of Rwanda, 2000), and is mirrored in all subsequent missions and programmes of the Ministry of Education (Republic of Rwanda, 2013a, p. 1) as: 'to *transform the Rwandan citizenry into skilled human capital for socio-economic development ... by ensuring equitable access to quality education*'. The policy strategy places strong emphasis on basic education, as part of the broader aspiration towards developing skilled human resources, through improving literacy and numeracy rates; promoting equal access to basic services, to training in skills, and thereby strengthening social cohesion.

These foundational government objectives were also conspicuously reiterated in subsequent education policy commitments and legislations, notably the Education Sector Policy of 2003; the Special Needs Education Policy of 2007; Laws of Rwanda relating to Protection of disabled persons in general of 2007; the Organic Law governing organisation of education of 2011; the Ministry of Education Nine Years Basic Education – goal Implementation-Fast Track Strategies of 2008; Girls' Education Policy of 2008; the five year Education Sector Strategic Plans (ESSP); Early Childhood Development Policy of 2011, and others (Republic of Rwanda, 2011a, 2011b, 2013a). For Example, the ESSP (Republic of Rwanda, 2013b) highlights the contexts for CwD' education within the next five years (2013–2018) as:

> The cross-cutting issue of equal access and participation of children with disabilities is one of the key challenges for the sector and has thus been prioritised as one of the ten strategic outcome areas for the ESSP ... A 7 to 8 year old child with disabilities is three times less likely to start school at the right age ... a child with disabilities has an 18% greater chance of repeating a primary school class ... and his or her chance of dropping out of school is four times higher than those of a child with no disabilities ... Not all schools and learning institutions are adequately equipped with appropriate facilities ... ensuring that all schools in Rwanda are Child-Friendly and Disabled-friendly is a challenge which has to be further addressed .... (pp. 11–25)

In view of the developments thus, the government commitments to educating CwD appears as a preoccupying feature across government social policies (Republic of Rwanda, 2000, 2005, 2011b, 2012). The Ministry of Gender and

Family Promotion's National Integrated Child Rights Policy (ICRP) for example, affirms that the Government recognises the special educational needs of children with various challenges, and will make possible efforts to include the children in mainstream schools where possible. It also pledges special support to ensure basic education for children who cannot be integrated in regular schools due to the severity of their disabilities (Republic of Rwanda, 2011b).

It is noted with interest in fact that the government of Rwanda seems to have actually defined its policy position with regards to education of all children in alignment with international social standards (DfID, 2000; Metts, 2000; Hoogeveen, 2005; Mont, 2007; Republic of Rwanda, 2013a, 2013b; WHO, 2013). It is on this prompting note that the next sections investigate the extent to which the policy strategies are actually working for inclusion of all Rwandan CwD in education, especially those in disadvantaged communities and schools.

3.6 *Planning Rwandan Children with Disabilities' Education*

Previous enquiries and experiences in the post-genocide Rwandan inclusive and special schools have noted trends and practices that inaccurately correspond with the country's policy stance and government programmes (Karangwa, 2000, 2001, 2004; Karangwa et al., 2007, 2010; Williams et al., 2014). On the contrary, they underline the course taken by locally-initiated inclusive and special school projects, as the preferred way forward despite their evident lack of links with the national policy trends (Handicap International, 2015; Karangwa, 2014; Karangwa et al., 2007, 2013). The African Decade for Disability (Rwanda Chapter) for example, reported that 90% of the 522,856 Rwandan people with disabilities are school age children and youths with disabilities (Republic of Rwanda, 2010b, p. 21), disagreeing radically with the data presented by the Ministry of Education and the Ministry of Economic Planning (Republic of Rwanda, 2015b, pp. 6–26) below:

> The population of Rwanda in 2014 is estimated at 11,002,631, and the majority of the learning population is enrolled in Primary level (71.4%) ... the number of children with disabilities enrolled in pre-primary school increased from 1,153 pupils in 2013 to 1,387 pupils in 2014 ... Pupils with disabilities represent 0.8% of 2,399,439 enrolled in primary education ... Students with disability represent 0.9% of 565,312 enrolled in Secondary education in 2014.

The clear controversy raised by the data is that though about 470, 570 youths (90%) are presented by a recognized Rwandan Non-Governmental Organizations (NGO) of people with disabilities as school-age (Republic of

Rwanda, 2010b), only 33, 000 (0.9% of all learners) are acknowledged by the Rwandan government education planning agencies (Republic of Rwanda, 2015b). The margin underlines a large number of CwD that are arguably unaccounted for, and are therefore, not planned for or likely to miss out in schooling and other basic services.

Equally, a critical glance at the Rwandan educational policy setting, it is easily construable that CwD are encouraged to access basic education alongside their peers despite the disadvantageous contexts in which inclusive and special needs education continues to be implemented. However, a close survey of situations in which teachers operate; the largely unformed parents' attitudes about their CwD's needs; situations of poor and scanty resources that renders schools functionally disempowered to maintain CwD; all raise doubts about effective and sustainable inclusion of CwD in many Rwandan schools.

Personal experiences since 1997 indicate steadily growing number of children with disabilities and other special educational needs accessing neighborhood basic schools, encouraged by the prevailing government programs and policy strategies, but an equally high dropout rate seems to ensue routinely (Karangwa, 2001, 2003, 2004, 2014; Karangwa et al., 2013). Children with disabilities are not necessarily barred from the free and compulsory 9YBE for example; however, the predominance of untrained educators; inappropriate teaching strategies; inadequate support services (rehabilitation, therapeutic and curricular provisions) as well as learning/ teaching environment and resources, all seem to contribute to early age dropout rate for many CwD. The Ministry of Education Statistical Yearbook report (Republic of Rwanda, 2015b, pp. 16–17) appears to agree with the discrepancy:

> Primary Net Enrolment Rate has increased from 95.4% in 2010 to 96.8% in 2014 which is close to 2014/2015 ESSP target of 98%, and 2017/2018 ESSP target of 100% … Much more effort is required to meet the 2017/2018 ESSP target of 75%. … the transition rate from Primary to Secondary school levels continues to decrease from 93.8% in 2010 to 73.4% in 2013, which is lower than the 2014/2015 ESSP target of 87.3% … a high repetition rate is observed in Primary one (25.7%), followed by Primary five (16.2%) while the lowest repetition rate is observed in Primary 6 (2.7%). A high dropout rate is observed in Primary Five (28.3%), followed by Primary two (13.8%) while the lowest dropout rate is observed in Primary one (10.2%).

It could as well be added that whereas the government education plans, especially the free and compulsory Nine Year Basic Education (9YBE) program explain the record high Enrolment Rate of 96.6% (Republic of Rwanda, 2011b), it is equally noted that children who are disadvantaged by their disabilities or other special educational needs constitute the high proportion of those who dropout or stagnate in schooling. Such situation is explained by Filmer's (2008, p. 141) surveys in developing countries, proving that the magnitude of school participation deficit associated with disability is as high as 50 percent, and is often larger than deficits related to other characteristics, such as gender, rural residence, or economic status differentials.

Having noted the rising number of centers for special education and rehabilitation around the country, the increased involvements of international organizations in inclusive and special needs education projects for the last ten years, it is understandable that the few children with disabilities (about 0.9%) recorded in Rwandan schools (Republic of Rwanda, 2015b) are actually likely be those in the ill-equipped special schools, and in about 55 ordinary schools striving to support few neighbourhood CwD (Handicap International, 2015). In fact, the few special and inclusive education initiatives that demonstrated innovative outcomes in education of Rwandan CwD, have reported more of individual and/or community inputs than government-supported accomplishments. Citing earlier reports on post-genocide Rwandan Inclusive education developments, Sue Stubbs' (2008) study on 'where there are few resources' observed that

> ... combined efforts of activists, the government, parents, teachers, and community members in post-genocide Rwanda ... a resource room for blind students, houses for volunteer staff, and a reading room were established ... African people have a well entrenched culture of family bonds, community solidarity and a spirit of mutual support – all of which should be exploited for the benefits of inclusion ... These blind students subsequently graduated from secondary school and began pressurizing for access to university ... Twenty-two students with visual, hearing and physical disabilities were enrolled in three universities. (p. 105)

Accordingly, the present study perceives great strides made in education policy and programmme designs that favour education of children with disabilities since 2003; however, it equally makes out strains and struggles of disadvantaged school teachers and parents, who are largely obscured from the government policy frameworks and strategies. In either case, it highlights perceivable innovations in some Rwandan schools and communities, as teachers and parents are condemned to addressing the educational needs of their CwD with available means and resources, as a forecast to latently developing Rwandan inclusive education initiatives.

4 Disability and Inclusive Education Developments in Rwanda

The situation surrounding children with disability and inclusive education in Rwanda like in the rest of the sub-region, is quite scantly explored by scholars (Karangwa et al., 2007; Stubbs, 2008; Talley et al., 2016), however, the next sections will strive to trace the key factors surrounding disability in Rwanda, investigating particularly the country's development trends that impact on the CwD's families and education.

4.1 *Disabling Factors and Development Trends*

The second Rwandan Economic Development and Poverty Reduction Strategy (EDPRS II 2013–2018) maintains that the country's post genocide adversities have progressively been turned into opportunities by creating the national "Vision 2020" strategies. It affirms that the development trends is experiencing one of the fastest socioeconomic strides towards achieving the middle income status, recording tenth fastest growing economy in the world during the decade 2000–2009, sustaining average GDP growth of 11.5% and reduction of poverty to less than 30% of the population (Republic of Rwanda, 2013b).

Accordingly, the picture of Rwanda's steady move out of disadvantaging contexts is indeed noticeable in terms of substantially improved infrastructure and a range of social services developed in the last ten years, and is certifiable by the author's personal experiences. However, given that poverty, disability and morbidity are inseparably intertwined cause and consequence of each other (DfID, 2000; Filmer, 2008; Hoogeveen, 2005; Metts 2000; Yeo & Moore, 2003), it is equally observed that despite the economic advances, poverty and disability seem to persist covertly within the Rwandan society, and continue to impact on the wellbeing of many families and their children's education in Rwanda (Talley et al., 2016; Williams et al., 2015). The DfID (2000, p. 3) Issues paper affirms for example, that the disabling factors that are directly linked to poverty (50% of which are preventable) include poor nutrition, dangerous working and living conditions, limited access to vaccination, health and maternity care programmes, poor hygiene, bad sanitation, inadequate information about the causes of impairments, war, accidents and natural disasters, and most of these are still noticeable in Rwanda.

On the one hand however, the 'over-generalised picture' projected by international agencies about disability in less developed countries could as well be treated with skepticism for they seems to deliberately ignore achievements made through improved health services in many of them include (Republic of Rwanda, 2013b); on the other, their analyses seem to serve as key pointers to realities that account for Rwanda's adverse situation of CwD's education

(GTZ, 2006; Filmer, 2008; WHO, 2013). EDPRS II 2013–2018 for one highlights the vicious cycle that significantly associates Rwanda's poverty and disability of children (Republic of Rwanda, 2013b):

> ... 44% of children under five years, and 47% of children under two years old suffer from chronic malnutrition (stunting) ... Chronically malnourished (stunted) children perform less well in school and are economically less productive as adults, ... risk losing 10% of their lifetime earning potential, ... and can cause the country to lose up to 3% of GDP ... Poverty and education levels, especially of the mother, are important factors for chronic malnutrition ... in some districts; the high levels of stunting can still not be fully explained ... 78% of children between 12–23 months are fed on low-nutrient diets. (pp. 84–85)

The assessments report goes on to reveal that though child mortality declined from 86 to 50 infant deaths per 1,000 live births, and maternal mortality from 750 to 476 per 100,000 between 2006 and 2011 (p. 7), many Rwandans (27%) still need more than an hour to reach the closest health facility (<5 km), and 12% of administrative sectors do not have any health center, while 15% of health centers have no electricity (p. 87). Besides, of the 73% households that have access to improved water sources (p. 106), the majority are in urban areas (about 92%) and are still limited in rural areas (about 69%). Only about 96% of Rwandan households have toilet facilities (especially outside the house), and about 42% of them use the bush as the main mode for sewage disposal (p. 85). It is noted that though the situation seems to be fast improving in urban areas, the conditions in rural areas and other disadvantaged communities where over 90% of Rwandans live remain in adverse conditions (Republic of Rwanda, 2012).

The desolate conditions to which the majority of Rwandan children's schools, communities and families are subjected, also suggest a glimpse on factors that influence their parents' and teachers' circumstances, and therefore, the means and attitudes with which they are able to support education of those with disabilities.

4.2 Cultural Perceptions and Education Planning

Reflecting on Loeba, Eide, and Mont's (2008, p. 33) affirmation that national disability prevalence rates around the world vary dramatically because ways societies perceive and assess disability also vary, it is equally learnt that education for Rwandan CwD is inadequately planned because it is largely understood from local cultural perspectives. Loeba et al. (2008) argue that despite the high prevalence of disabling factors, many African countries report low disability rates (below 5%) while high-income countries report high average (above 10%). The 2010 disability census conducted countrywide in collaboration with the Rwanda National Decade Steering Committee (Chapter of the African decade of Persons with disabilities) for example, revealed a total of 522,856 Rwandan Persons with Disabilities (263,928 females and 258,928 males) representing only 5.02% of the country's total population (Republic of Rwanda 2010b, pp. 8–15), a notably disability prevalence report likened to others in African countries (Altman, 2001; Loeba et al., 2006; Whyte & Ingstad, 1995).

Accordingly, the definition and prevalence of disability seems greatly dependent on the prevailing cultural contexts and may in turn have a significant impact on the services planned for CwD. The observation is made by Loeba et al. (2008, p. 34) about the 1990 Zambian disability census inadequacies, suggesting the focus shifts from measuring disability as a deviation from the normal, to assessments of difficulties encountered (both personal and environmental) and what an individual may need to become a fully active and integrated member of society, notably rehabilitation, education and professional training.

Like the Zambian experiences, the 2010 Rwandan disability census results (Republic of Rwanda, 2010b, p. 8) seem to be a reflection of the Rwandan perception of disability, rather than accurate measurements of individual functional potentials and contextual factors suggested by the World Health Organisation tools validated in a number of countries (WHO, 2001, p. 62, 2013, p. 6). It is actually noted with concerns that the World Health Organisation (WHO, 2013, p. 4) suggested paradigm shift to alternative disability assessment guidelines are clearly ignored by the Rwanda's Ministerial Order No. 20/18 of 27/7/2009 (Articles 2 and 3). The latter suggests modalities of classifying persons with disabilities in five categories only: Physically disabled; Sight-impaired; Deaf-and-dumb; Mentally disabled; and Persons with unspecified disabilities (Republic of Rwanda, 2010b, p. 15), which also characteristically depict the local translation of the categories in the Rwanda contexts. On the other hand, the WHO (2013, p. 8) defines disability in 10 categories from the perspective of ICF (International Categorisation of Functions), and organised in two parts: functioning and disability, and contextual factors.

As Loeba et al. (2008, p. 33) observe that 'achieving standardised, international consensus on disability issues is a challenging feature, and the idea of *'redefinition of cultural perceptions on disability'* to reflect *functional limitations* rather than impairments, is deemed more appealing in order to achieve more valid data with which governments can fittingly plan for their CwD's education.

4.3   *Disability in Education for National Development*

The perception of citizens with disabilities from the viewpoint of their potentials to participate in socio-economic developments is ostensibly still an obscure perspective to many African strategic planners including Rwandans (Hoogeveen, 2005; Metts, 2000; Mont, 2007; Shakespeare & Watson, 1997; Yeo, 2003). Therefore, the extent to which governments are able to plan CwD's education for subsequent participation in society, may actually depend on the level at which citizens with disabilities are perceived as indispensable potential contributors to development. According to Yeo's (2003) observations however, this is not yet the case in many African countries that include Rwanda:

> By all definitions of poverty, disabled people in developing countries are over-represented among the poor ... Social exclusion and isolation are a frequent part of their daily experience ... Often, the disabled are deprived of the opportunity to participate in productive work and thus become impoverished more easily than the rest of the population. Poverty also causes new disabilities as a result of poor and dangerous living conditions ... Poverty and disability reinforces each other, contributing to increased vulnerability and exclusion. (pp. 7–8)

In fact, studies conducted in Zambia Loeba et al. (2008, p. 33) and Rwanda Republic of Rwanda (2010b, p. 8) leave sufficient room to argue that cultural perceptions largely obscure and/or misdirect development plans at both macro and micro levels. The situation points to associated social and economic disadvantages in which Rwandans with disabilities are positioned, coined as a vicious circle of disability and poverty (Filmer, 2008; Karangwa et al., 2007; Metts, 2000). A similar context is reiterated by the Ministry of Local Government's census report, which also agrees that poverty is both a cause and effect of disability in Rwanda (Republic of Rwanda, 2010b, p. 8). It reaffirms that the genocide and war of 1990s contributed enormously to the rise in number and desolation of people with disability, and the displacement of people, destruction of homes, property and public services that ensued, overstressed their poverty conditions. Accordingly, the situation is even worsened by the fact that in matters of inheritance of land and other family assets, the disabled persons are often left to depend on other family members' support. This particularly affect those with severe disabilities (Intellectual disabilities, Blind and Deaf) for whom negative attitudes are particularly stronger (p. 7), and therefore are the most marginalised in basic services that include health care, education, training and therefore, discent living.

Pointing to poverty, disease and lack of medical care as the persistent sources of disability in the country, the report also reveals that Rwandan disabled people's potentials are underestimated, are predominantly objects of charity, and disabled females are even more disadvantaged socially and economically (p. 8). Accordingly, Rwandan CwD find it more difficult to attend school than non-disabled peers, and subsequently get training for competitive employment (Republic of Rwanda, 2013b, pp. 84–85). Arguably, the disadvantageous situation of Rwandans with disabilities renders them potential contributors to the country's underdevelopment, as affirmed by DiID (2004, p. 4) through the statement of James Wolfensohn, president of the World Bank.

Unless disabled people are brought into the mainstream of society, it will be impossible to cut poverty in half by 2015 or to give every child the chance to achieve primary education by the same date ... Disability needs to be brought to the development mainstream through a dynamic alliance of the UN system, governments, development agencies and other groups worldwide.

Metts' (2004, p. 8) study estimated the total annual GDP loss worldwide due to disability between $1.71 and $2.23 trillion or between 5.35% and 6.97% of the total global GDP, and estimates the annual GDP lost by Rwanda due to disability between 12.771% and 9.804% (pp. 36–38). It is learnt from the DfID (2000, p. 3) issues paper too that the cost of disability to families and communities has three components: *the direct cost of treatment, the indirect costs to family members who directly care for a member with a disability; and the opportunity costs of income foregone from incapacity*. In the absence of quantifiable explanations for Rwanda's disability factors therefore, studies (Filmer, 2008; Metts, 2000; Yeo, 2003) that characterise the situation as '*hidden cost of disability*' that accounts for the 'country's *hidden face of poverty*' appears also to explain the contextual for the large number of Rwandan CwD who miss in educational, rehabilitation and training services.

5 Discussions

Quite a number of issues that have important bearing to the education of CwD in Rwanda have been raised, and the next sections have been prompted to discuss key emerging features that seem to pertinently contribute to prospects of inclusive education in Rwanda.

5.1 The Background Influences
The education of Rwandan CwD has, for quite a long time been dependent on charity and benevolent support, and it is notable that even in the current

periods when the government has firmly defined its position and pledged its support (Republic of Rwanda, 2008a, 2011b, 2013a, 2013b), both special and inclusive education initiatives are still closely associated with charitable organizations. On one hand, it is not clear whether there is a link between the apparent inadequacies in education of Rwandan CwD and the persistent dependence of their education on charity and Non-Governmental organisations' support; on the other, in the face of the persistent inadequate response to Rwandan CwD's educational needs, it is understandable that individuals, social organisations and school-based projects are led to find own means to address issues of CwD. In this regard, Stubbs' (2008, p. 760) observation that 'ownership and attitude change go hand-in hand where there are few resources, and generate solutions in building inclusive education projects and programmes', ought to be taken as a complementing counsel to the evolving initiatives in Rwandan schools and communities.

5.2   *Defining Disability for Rwandan Education Planners*

The analyses in the previous sections brought to the surface the controversies that arise from Rwandans' definition of the concept '*Ubumuga*' or '*disability*', for it also interchangeably implies *impairment, disability* or *handicap* (Karangwa et al., 2007). It underlined the fact that the ways definitions are interpreted may also impact significantly on the ways policy missions and strategies are implemented (Shakespeare et al., 1997). The Rwandan government policy statements declares disability of citizens as a daunting socio-economic feature for example, and identifies quality education as the indisputable avenue through which citizens with disabilities are to be empowered for their ultimate participation in development (Republic of Rwanda, 2013a, 2013b). However, the approaches used to assess and translate disability-related strategies into relevant programs and services seem to be influenced by the local perceptions on disability, hence, are often dissatisfactory or disorient education planning and provisions.

The causes and effects of disability are abundantly present in the Rwandan contexts, and it is quite compelling to agree that a '*hidden cost of disability*' persists in Rwanda and accounts for the country's '*hidden face of poverty*' as maintained by Republic of Rwanda (2010b, 2013b); Metts (2000) and Yeo et al. (2003). Therefore, the vicious cycle of disability, vulnerability and poverty to which Rwandans with disabilities happen to be subjected, inevitably calls for integrated twin-tracked intervention strategies that include: education, training and Rehabilitation services on one hand, and enabling or sustained empowerment programmes on the other (Metts, 2000).

6 Conclusion: Prospects for Inclusive Education in Rwanda

Noting that though the drop-out rates in lower secondary education seem to have improved from 17.7% in 2012 to 14.7% in 2013 due to the Nine Year Basic Education (9YBE) programs that favored disadvantaged communities, both net and gross transition rates from primary to secondary schools seem to be decreasing from 41.5% in 2013 to 40.7% (gross) in 2014 and from 36.4% in 2013 to 35.7% (gross) in 2014, and CwD are most likely the main victims of the trend.

Accordingly, Rwanda ought to take heed of Filmer's (2008, p. 141) prediction of a worrisome vicious cycle that links low schooling attainment and subsequent poverty among people with disabilities in developing countries. However, though the pledged government commitments regarding education of CwD are often inadequately translated at implementation levels, the author foresees a future for education of CwD in less conventional and home-made avenues. The roles played by the annual national policy evaluation forum known as '*Umushyikirano*' for example, has been proven enormously significant. It brings together the head of state and representatives of all public and civil societies including citizens with disabilities, to publically assess achievements made in realizing development milestones set by the Seven Year Government programmes (7YGP 2010–2017), including its articles 194, 187 & 215 that regard services for people with disabilities and other special needs (Republic of Rwanda, 2010b). Some of the realizations in teacher training programmes in the University of Rwanda (UR) for example, were a direct result of persistent call for the realization of Article 215 in the 7YGP. The prospects are equally reflected in Stubbs' (2008, p. 105) observations of Rwandan inclusive education developments.

It is consequently hoped that the growing number of UR trained practitioners in special needs education and related services, stand out as one of the key prospects to count on for achieving CRPD targets. Mainly because the graduates are steadily finding their due space in education strategic planning at various levels and sectors, and will inevitably guide the service provisions towards appropriate standards that children with disabilities and other special needs duly deserve as a matter of constitutional right.

It is on the same note that the present study finds the Malaysian lesson from Jelas and Ali (2014) quite relevant to the developments in Rwanda's education of CwD. In their investigation of problematic issues associated with the interpretation of inclusive education policies into school and community-level practices, their findings concluded with suggestions of '*bifocal perspectives*' (p. 1001): one that focuses on redefinition of inclusive education policies and practices to suit both the social needs and international mandates; one that focuses on the social, cultural and educational traditions and philosophies, that are indigenous to local schools and the larger society. Accordingly, the lessons leant by the post-genocide Rwandans seems quite fundamental, for it impels cautious steps in advancing education programmes and projects, by identifying socio-political potholes, while harnessing socio-cultural leverages and potentials.

References

Altman, B. M. (2001). *Disability definitions, models, classification schemes and applications*. In G. L. Albrecht, K. D. Seelman, & M. Bury (Eds.), *Handbook of disability studies*. London: Sage Publications.

Braithwaite, J., & Mont, D. (2009). *Disability and poverty: A survey of World Bank poverty assessments and implications*. Washington, DC: Elsevier Masson.

Byanafashe, D., & Rutayisire, P. (2011). *Histoire du Rwanda. Des origines a la Fin du XXe Siecle*. Kigali: Commission Nationale pour l'Unité et la Réconciliation.

Christie, P. (2008). *Opening the doors of learning: Changing schools in South Africa*. Cape Town: Heinemann.

Cohen, L., Manion, L., & Morrison, K. (2003). *Research methods in education*. London: Routledge.

Denzin, N. K., & Lincoln, Y. (Eds.). (2000). *Discipline and practice of qualitative research: Handbook of qualitative research*. London: Sage Publications.

DfID. (2000). *Disability, poverty and development*. London: DfID.

Filmer, D. (2008). Disability, poverty, and schooling in developing countries: Results from 14 household surveys. *World Bank Economic Review, 22*(1), 141–163.

Goetz, J. P., & LeCompte, M. P. (1984). *Ethnography and qualitative design in educational research*. London: Academy Press.

GTZ. (2006). *Disability and development: A contribution to promoting the interests of persons with disabilities in German development cooperation*. Berlin: GIZ.

Guba, E. G., & Lincoln, Y. S. (1994). Competing paradigms in qualitative research. In N. K. Denzin & Y. S. Loncoln (Eds.), *Handbook of qualitative research* (pp. 105–117). Thousand Oaks, CA: Sage Publications.

Handicap International. (2015). *Paving the path to the success of inclusive education in Rwanda: Booklet 2*. Kigali, Rwanda.

Hoogeveen, J. (2005). Measuring welfare for small but vulnerable groups: Poverty and disability in Uganda. *Journal of African Economies, 14*, 603–631.

Jelas, Z. M., & Ali, M. M. (2014). Inclusive education in Malaysia. *International Journal of Inclusive Education, 18*(10), 991–1003.

Kalyanpur, M. (2008). Equality, quality and quantity: challenges in inclusive education policy and service provision in India. *International Journal of Inclusive Education, 12*(3), 243–262.

Karangwa, E. (2003). *Challenging the exclusion of blind students in Rwanda* (Enabling Education No 7). Manchester: EENET. Retrieved from http://www.eenet.org.uk/newsletters/news7/page4.shtml

Karangwa, E. (2008). *Inclusive higher education in Rwanda: The story continues* (Enabling Education No 12). Manchester: EENET.

Karangwa, E. (2014). Towards inclusive education in Rwanda: An assessment of the socio-political contributors to inclusive education developments. *Rwandan Journal of Education, 2*(1), 49–63.

Karangwa, E., Iyamuremye, D., & Muhindakazi, A. (2013). The plight of learners with visual disabilities in science classes. *Rwandan Journal of Education, 1*, 17–35.

Karangwa, E., & McGeown, J. (2013, September 10–13). *International agencies: What is their contribution to the future of inclusive education in Rwanda.* Paper presented at the UKFIET International Conference on Education and Development, Post 2015, Oxford.

Karangwa, E., Ghesquire, P., & Devlieger, P. (2007). The grassroots community in the vanguard of inclusion: The post-genocide Rwandan prospects. *International Journal of Inclusive Education, 11*, 607–626.

Loeba, M. E., & Eide, A. H. (2006). Paradigms lost: The changing face of disability in research. In B. Altman & S. Barnartt (Eds.), *International views on disability measures: moving towards comparative measurement* (Vol. 4, pp. 111–129). Oxford: Elsevier.

Loeba, M. E., Eide, A. H., & Mont, D. (2008). *Approaching the measurement of disability prevalence: The case of Zambia.* Washington, DC: Elsevier Masson.

Metts, L. R. (2000). *Disability issues, trends and recommendations for the World Bank.* Washington, DC: World Bank.

Mont, D. (2007). Measuring health and disability. *The Lancet, 369*, 1658–1663.

Republic of Rwanda. (2000). *Rwanda vision 2020.* Kigali: Ministry of Finance and Economic Planning.

Republic of Rwanda. (2003a). *The constitution of the Republic of Rwanda.* Kigali: Prime Minister.

Republic of Rwanda. (2003b). *Education sector policy.* Kigali: Ministry of Education.

Republic of Rwanda. (2005). *Strategic plan for street children.* Kigali: Ministry of Local Government.

Republic of Rwanda. (2007a). *Special needs education policy.* Kigali: Ministry of Education.

Republic of Rwanda. (2007b). *Codes and laws of Rwanda relating to protection of disabled persons in general.* Kigali: Ministry of Justice.

Republic of Rwanda. (2008a). *Ministry of education nine years basic education – Implementation-fast track strategies.* Kigali: Ministry of Education.

Republic of Rwanda. (2008b). *Girls education policy.* Kigali: Ministry of Education.

Republic of Rwanda. (2010a). *Republic of Rwanda government program 2010–2017.* Kigali: Prime Mister's Office.

Republic of Rwanda. (2010b). *Census of people with disabilities in Rwanda*. Kigali: Ministry of Local Government.

Republic of Rwanda. (2011a). *Early childhood development policy*. Kigali: Ministry of Education.

Republic of Rwanda. (2011b). *Mapping the ways forward: Planning for 12 year basic education*. Kigali: Ministry of Education.

Republic of Rwanda. (2012). *The fourth Rwanda Population and Housing Census (RPHC)*. Kigali: Ministry of Finance and Economic Planning.

Republic of Rwanda. (2013a). *Education sector strategic plan, 2013–2018*. Kigali: Ministry of Education.

Republic of Rwanda. (2013b). *Economic development and poverty reduction strategy II, 2013–2018*. Kigali: Ministry of Finance and Economic Planning.

Republic of Rwanda. (2015a). *The constitution of the republic of Rwanda of 24th December 2015*. Kigali: Prime Minister's Office.

Republic of Rwanda. (2015b). *Education statistical year book*. Kigali: Ministry of Education.

Shakespeare, T., & Watson, N. (1997). Defending the social model. *Disability and Society, 12*(2), 293–300.

Stubbs, S. (2008). *Inclusive education where there are few resources*. Oslo: Atlas Alliance.

Talley, L., & Brintnell, E. S. (2016). Scoping the barriers to implementing policies for inclusive education in Rwanda: An occupational therapy opportunity. *International Journal of Inclusive Education, 20*(4), 364–382.

WHO. (2001). *International classification of functioning, disability and health*. Geneva: World Health Organization.

WHO. (2013). *How to use the ICF: A practical manual for using the international classification of functioning, disability and health (ICF)*. Geneva: World Health Organization.

Whyte, S. R., & Ingstad, B. (1995). Disability and culture: An overview. In B. Ingstad & S. R. Whyte (Eds.), *Disability and culture*. London: University of California Press.

Williams, T., Abbott, P., & Mupenzi, A. (2015). Education at our school is not free': The Hidden costs of fee-free schooling in Rwanda. *Compare: A Journal of Comparative and International Education, 45*(6), 931–952.

Yeo, R., & Moore, K. (2003). Including disabled people in poverty reduction work: Nothing about us, without us. *World Development, 31*, 571–590.

Yeo, R. (2003). *Disability, poverty and the new development agenda*. London: Disability Knowledge and Research Programme, DFiD.

CHAPTER 3

Towards Inclusive Education Development: Addressing the Gap between Rhetoric and Practice in Zanzibar Schools

Said Juma

1 Introduction

The significance of inclusive education (IE) in improving the quality and equity of learning for all children has recently been reaffirmed in the Sustainable Development Goal 4 – 'ensure inclusive and quality education for all and promote lifelong learning' and in the Incheon Declaration for Education 2030 – 'towards inclusive and equitable quality education and lifelong learning for all' (UNESCO, 2015a). UNESCO Policy Guidelines on Inclusion in Education (2009, p. 4) describe IE as: '… a reform that supports and welcomes diversity amongst all learners' as well as: '… a process of strengthening the capacity of the education system to reach out to all learners (UNESCO, 2009, p. 8). At the core of IE is the process of combating educational and social exclusion by removing all barriers to learning and enabling all children to reach their full potential.

Combating exclusion is not, however, an easy process, because it has been deeply rooted in societies since time immemorial. Exclusion has been viewed as pervasive and elusive (Slee, 2011). It is ubiquitous and to achieve success towards inclusion, it should be viewed as everybody's business (Slee, 2011). As in many other countries in the Global North and South, exclusion in its various forms is still rampant in education systems.

The context of review in this chapter is Zanzibar, which is a semi-autonomous part of the United Republic of Tanzania off the East African coast. Zanzibar began to reform its education system towards IE in 2004 introducing IE as a project in 20 primary schools (McConkey & Mariga, 2011; Juma & Lehtomaki, 2016). However as of 2016, only about 30% of the government schools have been implementing IE (Murphy, Rawle, & Ruddle, 2016). Apart from this expansion several other measures have been taken to improve the implementation of IE practices in the schools. These measures include introduction of IE school committees in all the schools where IE was introduced, in-service training of teachers through teacher resource centres, education policy reforms in 2006, the process of developing inclusive education policy

© KONINKLIJKE BRILL NV, LEIDEN, 2019 | DOI:10.1163/9789004391505_004

(from 2010), establishment of a one-year course on IE at Zanzibar Muslim Academy and establishment of a two-year Diploma in Inclusive and Special Needs Education at the State University of Zanzibar (SUZA). In 2015, IE and life skills advisors and resource teachers who are based in the teacher resource centres located in all the 11 districts, were recruited. The Ministry of Education and Vocational Training (MoEVT) also appointed IE focal points from all the MoEVT departments in January 2017.

Using UNESCO's framework of inclusive, learning-friendly environments (UNESCO, 2015b), this review aims to find out what is really happening in Zanzibar schools as far as the implementation of IE is concerned. What are the strengths, gaps, opportunities and barriers to the implementation of the policy and other educational regulations regarding the IE process in Zanzibar? In this chapter, I address these questions through a critical analysis of the policies and the relevant documents to IE development in Zanzibar. Thereafter, I provide some recommendations, in relation to the UNESCO's framework, which will help in the implementation and further development of IE in the study context.

2   The Context and Development of Inclusive Education in Zanzibar

According to Zanzibar Education Master Plan 1996–2006, almost 90% of children aged 4 to 16 were enrolled in over 1, 700 *madrassas* (Koran schools) in Zanzibar. In these madrassas, children as young as three years of age gain early literacy skills and Islamic religious concepts. Some of these Koran schools have curricula which are internationally recognised through the support of The Aga Khan Foundation under the Madrasa Resource Centre. These Koran schools continue to provide religious education alongside formal primary and secondary schools. Thus most children in Zanzibar attend both Koran schools and the formal secular schools.

Formal education was declared free to all Zanzibaris after the 1964 revolution. However in later years from the 1990s due to economic hardships, a 'voluntary financial contribution' was introduced and private schools were reintroduced. The voluntary financial contribution for primary school pupils was abolished in 2015 during the 50th anniversary of the 1964 Revolution, when the president of Zanzibar announced the revival of free education policy starting from July 2015. In line with the Convention on the Rights of People with Disabilities, the Ministry of Education and Vocational Training (MoEVT) is the sole institution responsible for the education of all children.

The 2006 education policy reformed the structure of the formal education system whereby pre-primary education consisting of two years was made part of the basic and compulsory education followed by six years of primary schooling, four years of ordinary level secondary education (Forms I to IV), two years of advanced secondary education (Forms V to VI) and a minimum of three years of higher education. The entry age at pre-primary is four years, and at primary level is six years. Basic and compulsory education consists of 12 years (from pre-primary to ordinary level secondary). With regards to IE, the policy envisions striving for equitable access, quality education for all and promotion of lifelong learning. Through this policy, the government is committed to mainstreaming IE to all levels of education in Zanzibar. Among other things, the policy has introduced 12 years of basic and compulsory education. This is a great stride towards inclusive and learner-friendly education in Zanzibar as it will reduce the number of youth who are dropped out of the system of education after failing to pass their national Form II examinations. In addition, the policy now allows school girls who fall pregnant to resume studies after delivery. This step may reduce the number of girls who drop out because of becoming pregnant. The process of developing a distinct policy which is now called Zanzibar Inclusive Education Policy (2017 draft) is still in progress. In addition, Inclusive Education and Life Skills (IELS) Unit – the MoEVT's unit responsible for promoting IE in Zanzibar, in collaboration with external development partners such as Norwegian Association for Persons with Intellectual Disabilities (in Norwegian: *Norsk Forbund for Utviklingshemmede*, NFU) developed in 2015, a five-year strategic plan for IE implementation.

3   The Framework of Inclusive, Learning-Friendly Environments

UNESCO (2015b) defines an inclusive, learning-friendly environment as one which:

> … welcomes, nurtures, and educates all children regardless of their gender, physical, intellectual, social, emotional, linguistic, or other characteristics. They may be disabled or gifted children, street or working children, children of remote or nomadic peoples, children from linguistic, ethnic or cultural minorities, children affected by HIV/AIDS, or children from other disadvantaged or marginalized areas or groups. (p. 6)

It is: "child-friendly" and "teacher-friendly". It stresses the importance of students and teachers learning together as a learning community. It places children at the centre of learning and encourages their active participation in learning' (original emphasis, UNESCO, 2015b, p. 4).

Furthermore, UNESCO (2015b, p. 1) describes the inclusive, learning friendly-environment as consisting of five domains namely: (1) Proactively inclusive, seeking out and enabling participation of all children and especially those who are different ethnically, culturally, linguistically, socio-economically, and in terms of ability; (2) academically effective and relevant to children's needs for life and livelihood knowledge and skills; (3) Healthy and safe for, and protective of, children's emotional, psychological, and physical well-being; (4) Gender-responsive in creating environments and capacities fostering equality; and (5) Actively engaged with, and enabling of, student, family, and community participation in all aspects of school policy, management, and support to children.

Inclusive, learning-friendly environment framework is based on a number of learning theories such as Vygotsky's (1978) Sociocultural Theory. The theory describes learning as a social process determined by social interactions between the learner and the teacher or the more experienced peer. The framework is also based on the social model of learning difficulties and disabilities (Booth & Ainscow, 2002) which views disability as resulting from interactions between a person with a disability and the surrounding socio-cultural and political environment. The attitudinal, environmental and institutional barriers that are deeply inherent within society systematically exclude and marginalise people with disabilities. This chapter discusses the extent to which the educational practices in Zanzibar are in line with this UNESCO's inclusive, learning-friendly environment framework and provides recommendation for further improvement towards creating inclusive, learning friendly environment in Zanzibar schools.

4 Key Issues

4.1 *Demystifying Inclusion*
The Zanzibar Inclusive Education Policy (ZIEP) draft (2017) has adopted a broad definition of IE as: 'Education where all learners study together with other learners of their age in their community, irrespective of their abilities or disabilities; socio-economic, cultural or ethnic background; language; religion or gender' (ZIEP, [2017 draft]). Though the policy definition is in line with the UNESCO's framework by addressing all learners and not just those with disabilities, this understanding has not been internalised by teachers, parents, students and even some educational officers at ministerial level (NFU, 2014). In Zanzibar, as in many other countries, the shift in thinking towards inclusion has not, as yet, taken place. Still the focus and centre of discourse for many are

on disabilities and special educational needs (SEN) rather than all children. Focussing on all children is at the centre of the inclusive, learning friendly environment framework.

There has been too a tension between the fundamental principle of IE which views education system to be a problem rather than a child, and the argument that there are 'barriers within the child'. Although the policy is very clear about the social model of disability and learning difficulties that the child is not a problem but rather the education system, the practice and discourse among the practitioners are in tension. Some teachers still talk and argue that apart from the barriers in the system; there are also 'barriers within the child', which reflects the medical model viewing the child as a problem. This view results in focussing attention on a single track of meeting the learner's needs and leaving the wider and systemic issues within the education system and society as a whole. This situation leads to focussing attention on children with SEN especially those with disabilities forgetting other systemic issues such as drop outs, never enrolled children, corporal punishment, fear of bullying or violence, distance to school or lack of safe transport to and from school, heavy teacher workload, and unfamiliar language of instruction (UNICEF, 2006). It may also lead to focus attention on their differences and weaknesses, or what they have and do not have in lieu of their capabilities and strengths.

IE definitely does not ignore the fact that some children with disabilities have additional support needs. Hence a twin-track approach i.e. concurrently identifying and addressing the children's individual needs, and at the same time working to improve the whole system of education towards better presence (access), participation and achievement for all children (Enabling Education Network, 2013) is fundamental to building inclusive and learning-friendly environments.

The tension in a lack of clear understanding and conceptualisation of IE is further noted in ZEP (2006) and the ZIEP (2017 draft). There appears to be inconsistency and contradiction of the terms used in these two policy documents. While the latter cites an example of labelling by using terms such as 'lazy or slow learners' as being disrespectful, the former, which is the mainstream policy, paradoxically mentions 'slow learners' in a posit ive way:

> Slow learners and highly gifted children shall be identified and be given opportunities to learn at their own pace. (ZEP, 2006, p. 19)

Due to the lack of a bigger picture of inclusion, some teachers and educational officers associate IE only with children with disabilities. Thus, to avoid labelling children with disabilities, they still, in a way, unwittingly label them as 'inclusion children'. As Fullan (2005, p. 67) notes that 'terms travel easily ... but the meaning of the underlying concepts does not'. Definitely, such labelling may lead to perpetuating a notion that these children are qualitatively different from the others and hence teachers' expectations on these children will be low and the children may develop low self-esteem. IE requires an environment which is 'healthy and safe for, and protective of, children's emotional, psychological, and physical well-being' (UNICEF, 2006, p. 1). Teachers need to develop high expectations for all children at school, regardless of their background or (dis) ability, and support them in their learning process in order to achieve to their full potential. Thus IE aims to protect all children from exclusion both *from* and *within* education systems.

This tension echoes with those who argue that special education and IE are epistemologically irreconcilable (Allan, 2005). Regarding such tensions, Pather (2007) argues that there is a need to demystify the meaning of the term inclusion to the key implementers of IE such as teachers, parents and education officers. In simple terms, Pather (2007) further contends, inclusion means change. This change involves an on-going reflective process towards an environment where all learners can achieve. However, it important to note that this change does not happen overnight. Therefore, inclusion in the context of education should simply be understood as an evolutionary, rather than revolutionary change towards more equitable and quality learning.

4.2 'The Burden of Educating the Uneducable'?

The Zanzibar Education for All Assessment 2001–2013 shows that IE has not been fully accepted by some head teachers as they feel it is an extra burden for them (UNESCO, 2015c). This suggests that these head teachers only focus on the 'burden' of accommodating children with disabilities whom they believe are 'uneducable' by ordinary teachers and that these children need special education teachers or even special schools. It also suggests that in practice head teachers narrowly view IE as focussing on including children with disabilities into regular schools rather than an overall process of combating all barriers to learning, increasing and improving outcomes for all learners regardless of their diverse backgrounds and abilities. As Slee (2009, p. 180) notes the development of IE 'is not a linear narrative of progress toward enlightenment'. It involves embracing and cherishing diversity as well as adapting the curriculum to fit each child's abilities (Mitchell, 2014). Head teachers and other educational managers need to be exposed to the philosophy and practices of IE so that they can be convinced to work together with teachers to mobilise parents, community members, and other professionals to support them in creating inclusive and learning-friendly environments for all children.

4.3 *Exclusion through the Language of Instruction?*

The language of instruction (LoI) is crucial for meaningful learning especially during the early years. For many years before the introduction of ZEP (2006), Zanzibar used to be exemplary along with MainlandTanzania (Kiswahili), Somalia (Somali), Ethiopia (Amharic), and Eritrea (Tigrinya) in the Sub-Saharan Africa for using mother tongue language as LoI for the entire duration of primary education i.e. from pre-primary throughout primary level (Standard [Grade] I to Standard VII) unlike many other African countries. As Ouane, and Glanz, (2010) note, in Africa the majority of children begin school using an unfamiliar language. Zanzibar as a predominantly mono-ethnolinguistic community is graced with Kiswahili – a language understood and used virtually by all Zanzibaris. Nevertheless, the ZEP (2006) replaced Kiswahili as LoI for mathematics and science from Standard V.

This change of LoI has several implications for IE. Maalim (2015), has critically analysed the ZEP on the issue of LoI and has argued that the policy moved from being complimentary to contradictory. The policy seems to be in tension as teachers cannot implement it instead, they have resorted to Kiswahili and use English only in writing notes for students and in setting examination questions (Maalim, 2015). Thus English as LoI for the last two years of primary education in Zanzibar schools seems to remain merely a policy on paper and teachers find it difficult to fully implement it.

Apart from Maalim's, there are several other studies which reveal the tension in the LoI in Zanzibar schools (Babaci-Wilhite, 2012, 2013a, 2013b, 2014a, 2014b, 2015; Babaci-Wilhite & Geo-Jaja, 2011; Brock-Utne, 2013; Halai & Rea-Dickinks, 2013; Juma & Lehtomäki, 2015). Arguing along similar lines, Alidou and Brock-Utne (2011); and Vuzo (2010) contend that when learners are taught in a language they are unfamiliar with, they tend to be reluctant to freely interact with the teachers, ask or answer questions. Real teacher-student interactions are restricted when there is no common familiar language between the teacher and students in the classroom. In such classrooms, didactic and ritualistic pedagogical practices tend to govern the teaching process resulting into narrow meaningful learning experiences among the learners.

Heugh et al. (2007) also found that in Ethiopia, school pupils learning in their mother tongue performed better in mathematics, biology, chemistry and physics than pupils in English-medium schools. Brock-Utne (2013) further critiques the ZEP (2006) on the issue of changing the LoI as both disempowering and unnecessary because Kiswahili is the mother tongue of almost all teachers and all students in Zanzibar. Using English as LoI in Zanzibar is challenging not only to the students but also to the teachers. Hence, although language issues are discussed in the mainstream ZEP (2006), the efficiency of using English as LoI for science and mathematics remains very much in question as far as literature on LoI in Zanzibar context is concerned. The Zanzibar Inclusive Education Policy (2017 draft), however, does not highlight the LoI issue.

Looking through the lens of IE and especially the framework of inclusive, learning-friendly environments, the Zanzibar LoI policy may exclude some learners and negatively affect the provision of inclusive and learner-friendly education as envisaged in the policy. If pupils do not understand the LoI, they will have to memorise the notes and reproduce them during examinations leading to rote learning, and *banking* approach (Freire, 1970). If learners cannot freely access information or communicate their ideas due to a language barrier, how then can they engage in meaningful learning and experiences? Hence, learning by using a familiar language especially at elementary level, is necessary for ensuring an inclusive and learning-friendly environment in schools (Rea-Dickins & Yu, 2013; UNESCO, 2015b).

4.4   *Are Private Schools Supportive of the Policy?*
According to ZEP (2006, p. 36) 'private schools shall seek permission to use other languages as media of instruction'. However, one may wonder what criteria are in place to permit the private schools in Zanzibar to use English as LoI even at pre-primary level. If private sector continues to be the main provider of pre-primary education, what are the implications of this situation? This means that pupils from government schools will be from mostly Kiswahili medium schools and those from private schools are from the so-called English-medium schools. Whilst pupils in the government schools use Kiswahili as LoI from pre-primary to Standard IV, those in private schools use English as LoI throughout pre and primary education. After that, they all meet up at secondary and tertiary levels where English is the LoI. This situation creates inequalities among the students when they join secondary schools. My concern here is with regards to the target of ensuring that all girls and boys complete free, equitable and quality primary and secondary education as stipulated in the UN Sustainable Development Goal 4 (UNESCO, 2015a).

Furthermore, these private schools, more often than not, use interviews usually conducted in English! to predetermine the academic ability of students and charge fees poor families cannot afford to pay. Also, there has been a tendency in these schools to screen students prior to the registration in the national examinations such that those who seem to be unlikely to pass the national examinations are asked to repeat the year, move to a different school or register for the national examinations as 'private' instead of 'school' candidates. Hence these schools tend to be elitist by favouring those who can afford to pay and those who learn faster than others. This tendency definitely is not compatible with the UNESCO's inclusive, learning friendly environment framework.

Another issue is that although the establishment of private schools has helped to widen access to education among Zanzibari children, most of these schools cluster in the Urban West region and not necessarily accessible to the poor families who cannot afford the fees. Greater market viability and ability to pay in the Urban West region than in rural areas is possibly the reason for this concentration. Thus viewing from an IE lens private schools tend to widen social inequalities (Forlin, 2013). This is because only the well-off families can afford to send their children to the schools and only those who are likely to pass the national examinations can complete their studies in these schools. Thus they are not actually open to all children. In addition to excluding children from poor families, these schools may be reluctant to enrol students with special educational needs or those with disabilities. If not well handled, private schools may foster elitism and inequality rather than being supportive of the Zanzibar Inclusive Education Policy's vision of providing inclusive and learner-friendly education in Zanzibar.

4.5   *Distribution of the Policy Documents*

Zanzibar has made great strides in terms of enactment and review of policies to promote inclusion. Apart from the 2006 education policy reforms, the process of writing the ZIEP started in 2010. However, there appears to be a gap in policy advocacy as the majority of the teachers in schools are not aware what the policies say about IE development in Zanzibar. Although the ZEP (2006) has been translated into Kiswahili the document has not been adequately distributed. While teachers seem to be extremely busy occupied with teaching load, they do not seem to have time to read the documents especially when the documents are in an unfamiliar language.

Thus there is a need to engage teachers, who are the key implementers of the educational policies, in dialogue on inclusion by providing them easy to understand and abridged versions of the key policy documents in Kiswahili. Engaging teachers in dialogue around inclusion and creation of inclusive and learning-friendly school environments, if well-structured and supported, may be a means to shift teachers' understandings of what inclusion means, and increase their capacity to implement policy and create inclusive, learning-friendly environments in their respective schools (Robinson, 2017; UNICEF, 2006).

4.6 Strengths and Gaps in Protecting the Educational Rights of the Girl Child

The Protection of Spinster and Single Parent Act (Act 4 of 2005) section 4(2) consents girls suspended for a pregnancy to be reinstated to school in the next academic year or any time deemed to be most appropriate by the education authority but in any case, the suspension should not exceed two academic years. According to this provision, the school girls who fall pregnant may resume studies, under certain conditions.

Although the 2006 policy reforms include the re-entry policy for the school girls who fall pregnant, there is a gap in the enforcement of the policy. The Zanzibar Education Act No.6 of 1982 (Amended in 1993) section 20 (4), provides expulsion penalty for both a female pupil found to be pregnant before completing primary or junior secondary education and a male pupil found to be responsible for the pregnancy. With virtually over ten years since the launching of ZEP (2006), the act has not been amended again to enforce the implementation of the 2006 policy reform.

Furthermore, fighting against the causes of early marriages and teenage pregnancies is what should receive more attention. It is not enough to allow the girls to resume studies after delivery if there are no effective measures to reduce or eliminate such cases. Also, there is a pressing need to tackle the underlying reasons for the perpetrators continuing to impregnate school girls. The policies and research documents reviewed do not seem to pay much attention to this issue.

While quantitatively gender parity is not a big problem in basic education in Zanzibar (EMIS, 2014), there is still a lot to be done towards creating qualitative gender-friendly learning environments, which is a crucial aspect of the UNESCO's inclusive learning-friendly environment framework in creating gender-responsive learning environments and fostering equality among all learners.

4.7 Strengths and Tensions in Pre-Primary Schools

As a result of the 2006 education policy reforms, which made pre-primary education part of the basic and compulsory education in Zanzibar, there has been a rapid expansion of enrolment in pre-primary schools. However, there is a huge shortage of teachers who are qualified to teach at this level (EMIS, 2014; Murphy, Rawle, & Ruddle, 2016; UNESCO, 2015c). The basic assumption is probably that teachers with qualification to teach at primary level are also qualified to teach at pre-primary. This is pedagogically ineffective and impracticable. Pre-primary education requires more care to psychologically prepare the children for school than actually 'teach' them. It is a very important period of transition to formal schooling. It needs to be an inclusive transition to the next level.

The only formal training for pre-primary school teachers so far is offered by the Madrasa Resource Centre which is run by the Aga Khan Foundation. Recently (2015), over 10 years since the ZEP was approved, SUZA, which is the sole government institution responsible for teacher training as stipulated in the ZEP (2006), started to offer a two-year Diploma in Early Childhood Development (ECD). The Zanzibar Muslim Academy is planning to offer a one year course on ECD for pre-service teachers in the near future. There is therefore a gap here between policy and resources. Both human and material resources are not available for the implementation of this policy. Such resources are crucial in enabling inclusive, learning friendly environment at this foundation level of education.

My discussion with teacher resource centre advisors during a workshop on IE held at a teacher centre in Zanzibar in February 2016 revealed that teachers in some primary schools segregate between children with pre-school experience and those without such experience when they begin Standard I. This streaming may lead to increase in vulnerability to early repetition among children without pre-school experience (Office of Chief Government Statistician, 2013).

The impact of streaming, far from being to direct resources to the children who need them most, is to direct resources towards children already performing at a high level in relation to curriculum goals (Angelides, Charalambous, & Vrasidas, 2004). This issue may reinforce social inequalities as children whose families cannot afford to pay for private pre-primary schools are immediately disadvantaged. This practice is pedagogically destructive and may lead to the risk of the negative teacher self-fulfilling prophecy on the pupils they believe fall behind the others. Teachers may have low expectation from those children without pre-school foundation which in turn may lead to the risk of repetition and dropping out. This practice is contrary to IE principles, which oppose the practice of streaming school children on the basis of ability. Research has shown that mixed-ability teaching i.e. teaching of children with varying abilities in the same classroom and paying attention to the individual or small group differences is more effective than separating them according to their abilities (Angelides, Charalambous, & Vrasidas, 2004).

Another tension at pre-primary level is about the entry age. ZEP (2006) directs schools to enrol children aged four years to pre-primary schools. However, so far the major provider of pre-primary education has been the private sector (Murphy, Rawle, & Ruddle, 2016). Some private schools enrol pupils for three years before joining Standard I while the government schools have a two-year programme. This gap is noted by Statistical Abstract (2013, p. 3). This gap has implications to delayed entry into Standard I for some children. According to Murphy, Rawle, and Ruddle (2016) only 11% of Standard I pupils are enrolled at the right age. Delayed entry into primary schools may partly be associated with dropping out in the later years.

Data from Educational Management Information System (EMIS) (2012–2014) show a gap between government and private schools with regard to Standard I pupils who attended pre-school (UNESCO, 2015c). While the gross enrolment rate for pre-primary has increased from 30.1% in 2015 to 58.2% in 2016, MoEVT budget speech (2015/2016) indicates that enrolment in pre-schools is higher (55%) in private schools than in government schools. As private sector is the major provider of pre-primary education, enrolment in pre-primary school is still low. The situation is worse for children with disabilities due to factors such as negative attitude to disability. Review of the Zanzibar Education Development Programme 2008/2009–2015/2016 (Kundi & Mohammed, 2016) notes that parents have not been sensitized enough on the introduction of the ZEP which wants parents to send their four-year-olds to pre-schools. The Report further reveals that parents prefer their younger children to have adequate time to attend Koran schools before the formal primary schooling.

Moreover, there is a tension in pre-school curriculum content and the real-life situation in the classrooms. The number of subjects for pre-primary and primary school children is relatively big. It needs to be reduced. It is surprising that children right at pre-primary level have quite a big number of subjects and have to sit for oral and written examinations! Currently, there are seven subjects (Kiswahili, English, Arabic, Islamic religion, Science, Arts and Mathematics, at pre-primary level and 12 subjects namely Kiswahili, English, Arabic, Islamic religion, Geography, History, Civics, Information and Computer Technology, Physical education, Science, Mathematics, and Social science at primary level. It is assumed that pupils in Standard I have the pre-primary foundation, which is not usually the case for many pupils. As a result, teachers in some primary schools sort and stream Standard I pupils according to their background in pre-primary education.

4.8 *IE in Technical and Vocational Education and Training*

The analysis of the documents in this review shows that IE has not permeated to technical and vocational education and training institutions in Zanzibar. For example, ZEP (2006, p. 22) reveals that: 'technical and vocational education does not cater for the needs of students with special education needs'. This suggests that IE is so far only introduced in some primary and secondary schools and hence there is a gap of IE practices in vocational and technical training institutions. Including technical and vocational education institutions in inclusive education is particularly important because IE takes a broader view of education. Hence academic and vocational institutions as well as both formal and informal educational institutions need to get clear and consistent messages and orientation around IE.

4.9   *Preparing and Supporting Teachers for Inclusion*

Teacher training and continuing teacher professional development for inclusion are crucial for a successful implementation of IE (Booth & Dyssegaard, 2014). The documents reviewed discuss the importance of teacher training and continuing professional development but they do not specifically refer to IE. Although national policy and syllabi have changed to accommodate IE, teacher training and teacher education are lagging behind in preparing and developing teachers to provide learner-friendly education for all. As such, Zanzibar, like many other countries, appears to be strong on policy development but weak on policy implementation.

According to ZEP (2006, p. 44) all government teacher training colleges are to merge with the SUZA. Thus, it is high time SUZA reviewed the curriculum for pre-service teacher training including its mode of teaching practice to ensure that all student teachers are well prepared to effectively manage diversity in their classrooms by using inclusive pedagogy. This initiative is crucial towards reaching Sustainable Development Goal 4 and towards inclusive, learning friendly environments in all schools.

4.10   *Inclusive Transition*

As IE advocacy has so far concentrated on primary schools in Zanzibar, there are tensions during the transition from primary to secondary classes. As IE education training for in-service teachers is mostly focussing primary schools (Juma & Lehtomaki, 2016), the majority of the teachers in secondary schools are not orientated to IE, and are not capable of supporting the children who used to receive additional support from their primary schools teachers. This also applies to the difficulty such children face when they move from one school to another because of any reason. It is not any neighbourhood school that children with disabilities or those who need additional support in their learning can go. Some schools in Zanzibar are inaccessible and their teachers may not be well informed about the need for creating inclusive, learning friendly-environment for all children. Hence there is a gap of effective planning for inclusive transition from primary to secondary school level especially among children who might need additional support for their learning including those with disabilities or special educational needs.

5 Conclusions and Recommendations

In this chapter, I have critically reviewed documents related to the implementation of IE in Zanzibar in light of UNESCO's inclusive, learning-friendly environment framework consisting of inclusion; effectiveness; health, safety and protection; gender-responsiveness; and teamwork involving students, families, and communities. The review has shown that Zanzibar has made great strides in the process of implementing IE by introducing re-entry policy for school girls who fall pregnant, increasing the number of compulsory education from 10 to 12 years, abolishing school fees and making pre-primary as part of the basic and compulsory education. Also the development of IE policy is in progress. Despite this success, the review has revealed some gaps and weaknesses towards the realization of inclusive and learner-friendly education.

The need to review curriculum for both pre-primary and primary education to ensure an inclusive and learning-friendly environment in which all children can actively participate and achieve is worth considering. Also, the language policy with regards to the LoI needs further research. Teacher training and teacher professional development and support strategies need to reflect IE by supporting teachers to improve their pedagogical skills and practices. Engaging teachers in policy dialogue around IE may be a means of highlighting the centrality of inclusion to all school practices.

Speeding up the finalization of the ZIEP and development of operational guidelines to make sure that the policy is swiftly implemented is an important way forward towards ensuring inclusive and learning-friendly schools that can enhance learning for all children. Without adequate strategies for the preparation of and regular professional support for teachers, IE cannot be a reality. These strategies may include promoting reflective critical thinking skills among teachers through collaborative action research and teamwork.

Significant additional attention needs to be given to pre-primary and pre-school education in relation to primary education and to the development of transition programmes with effective parent involvement in the schools. The MoEVT should consider expanding its involvement and support of training, co-ordination to the Koran schools and the formal pre-primary schools in order to ensure quality provision of pre-primary education to all children. As these institutions enrol children at a very young age, there is a need for the MoEVT and Ministry of Health to monitor and support the improvement of the quality of child care, pre-school and pre-primary education. Better co-ordination between the MoEVT and the Ministry of Health is vital in building the foundation for a strong education system that works better for all rather than some children. Also, the MoEVT should increase budget allocation to its

IELS Unit in order to reduce dependency on external funding in running IE related activities.

In line with the inclusive and learning-friendly framework, mobilising community resources through school-community partnership is also needed for teachers, family, and community participation to support learning for all children. Reviving the IE school committees by clearly defining their composition, roles and functions, for example, may contribute to improving inclusion practice and creating a learning-friendly environment at the school level. A strong school-community partnership will enhance ownership of IE development process by the Zanzibar society and will not be viewed as a 'project' with heavy dependence on external funding. The process of creating inclusive, learning friendly environment in Zanzibar schools cannot be accomplished by the MoEVT alone. It requires a concerted approach of all educational stakeholders including parents, teachers, NGOs and other ministries of the Zanzibar government.

References

Alidou, H., & Brock-Utne, B. (2011). Teaching practices – Teaching in a familiar language. In A. Ouane & C. Glanz (Eds.), *Optimising learning, education and publishing in Africa: The language factor. A review and analysis of theory and practice in mother-tongue bilingual education in Sub-Saharan Africa* (pp. 159–185). Hamburg/ Tunis: UNESCO Institute for Lifelong Learning/Association for the Development of Education in Africa.

Allan, J. (2005). Inclusion as an ethical project. In S. Tremain (Ed.), *Foucault and the government of disability* (pp. 281–297). Ann Arbor, MI: The University of Michigan Press.

Angelides, P., Charalambous, C., & Vrasidas, C. (2004). Reflections on policy and practice of inclusive education in pre-primary schools in Cyprus. *European Journal of Special Needs Education, 19*(2), 211–223.

Babaci-Wilhite, Z. (2012). A right based approach to Zanzibar's language-in education policy. Special issue on right based approach and globalization in education. *World Studies in Education, 13*(2), 17–33.

Babaci-Wilhite, Z. (2013a). An analysis of debates on the use of a global or local language in education: Tanzania and Malaysia. In D. B. Napier & S. Majhanovich (Eds.), *Education, dominance and identity* (pp. 121–133). Rotterdam, The Netherlands: Sense Publishers.

Babaci-Wilhite, Z. (2013b). The new education curriculum in Zanzibar: The rationale behind it. In Z. Desai, M. S. A. Qorro, & B. Brock-Utne (Eds.), *The role of language in teaching and learning science and mathematics: LOITASA phase two research* (pp. 127–151). Cape Town: African Minds.

Babaci-Wilhite, Z. (2014a, July 14). *New perspective on language & literacy in Africa and Asia*. A Lead Paper Presented at the 17th Annual National Conference of the Association for Promoting Nigerian Languages and Cultures, Owerri, Nigeria.

Babaci-Wilhite, Z. (Ed.). (2014b). *Giving space to African voices: Right in local languages and local curriculum* (Vol. 33, pp. 1–217). Rotterdam, The Netherlands: Sense Publishers.

Babaci-Wilhite, Z. (2015). *Local language of instruction as a human right in education: Cases from Africa* (Vol. 36, pp. 1–154). Rotterdam, The Netherlands: Sense Publishers.

Babaci-Wilhite, Z., & Geo-JaJa, M. A. (2011). A critique and rethink of modern education in Africa's development in the 21st century. Papers in Education and Development (PED). *Journal of the School of Education, 30,* 133–154.

Booth, T., & Ainscow, M. (2002). *Index for inclusion: Developing learning and participation in schools*. Bristol: Centre for Studies on Inclusive Education.

Booth, T., & Dyssegaard, B. (2014). *The contribution of inclusive values to the development of education for all*. Retrieved January 30, 2016, from http://www.eenet.org.uk/resources/docs

Braun, V., & Clarke, V. (2006). Using thematic analysis in psychology. *Qualitative Research in Psychology, 3*(2), 77–101.

Brock-Utne, B. (2012). Language policy and science: Could some African countries learn from some Asian countries? *International Review of Education, 58*(4), 481–503.

EMIS. (2014). *MoEVT annual education statistical data*. Zanzibar.

Enabling Education Network (EENET). (2013). *Enabling education review, issue 2*. Retrieved January 31, 2015, from http://www.eenet.org.uk

Forlin, C. (2013). Changing paradigms and future directions for implementing inclusive education in developing countries. *Asian Journal of Inclusive Education, 1*(2), 19–32.

Freire, P. (1970). *Pedagogy of the oppressed*. London: Penguin Books.

Fullan, M. (2005). Professional learning communities' writ large. In R. DuFour, R. Eaker, & R. DuFour (Eds.), *On common ground: The power of professional learning communities* (pp. 209–223). Bloomington, IN: Solution Tree.

Heugh, K., Benson, C., Bogale, B., & Yohannes, M. (2007). *Study on medium of instruction in primary schools in Ethiopia: Final report*. Ethiopia: Commissioned by the Ministry of Education.

Juma, S., & Lehtomäki, E. (2016). Moving towards Inclusion: How Zanzibar succeeds in transforming its education system? *International Journal of Inclusive Education, 20*(6), 1–12.

Kundi, B., & Mohammed, S. (2016). *Ministry of Education and Vocational Training (MoEVT). Zanzibar Education Development Programme (ZEDP) (2008/09–2015/16)*. Retrieved from http://planipolis.iiep.unesco.org/upload/Tanzania

Lichtman, M. (2012). *Qualitative research in education: A user's guide.* London: Sage Publications.

Maalim, H. A. (2015). The replacement of Swahili medium of instruction by English from grade 5 in Zanzibar: From complementary to contradictory. *Nordic Journal of African Studies, 24*(1), 45–62.

McConkey, R., & Mariga, L. (2011). Building social capital for inclusive education: Insights from Zanzibar. *Journal of Research in Special Educational Needs, 11*(1), 12–19.

Ministry of Education. (1982). *The Zanzibar education act no.6.* Zanzibar: Government Printer.

Ministry of Education. (1996). *The Zanzibar education master plan 1996–2000.* Zanzibar. Government Printer.

Ministry of Education and Vocational Training Zanzibar (MoEVT). Budget speech *2013/2014.*

Mitchell, D. (2014). *What really works in special and inclusive education: Using evidence-based teaching strategies* (2nd ed.). Abingdon: Routledge.

MoEVT (Ministry of Education and Vocational Training). (2006). *Zanzibar education policy.* Retrieved January 20, 2016, from http://moez.go.tz/docs/pwA4nrszmk_Zanzibar_Education_Policy.pdf

MoEVT (Ministry of Education and Vocational Training) Zanzibar Inclusive Education Policy (2017 draft).

MoEVT (Ministry of Education and Vocational Training). (2015/2016). *Budget speech 2015/2016.*

Murphy, P., Rawle, G., & Ruddle, N. (2016). *Zanzibar education situation analysis: Final report.* Retrieved August 20, 2016, from http://moez.go.tz/eLab/docs/FinalReport-KeyFindingsBoxes_sent.pdf

NFU (Association of Persons with Developmental Disabilities). (2014). *Report on evaluation of the supported inclusive education project in Zanzibar.* Oslo.

Office of Chief Government Statistician Zanzibar. (2013). *Zanzibar statistical abstract 2012.* Zanzibar. Office of Chief Government Statistician.

Ouane, A., & Glanz, C. (2010). *Why and how Africa should invest in African languages and multilingual education.* Hamburg: UNESCO Institute for Lifelong Learning. Retrieved September 15, 2016, from http://www.campaignforeducation.org/docs/reports

Pather, S. (2007). Demystifying inclusion: Implications for sustainable inclusive practice. *International Journal of Inclusive Education, 11*(5–6), 627–643. doi:10.1080/13603110600790373

Pather, S., & Nxumalo, C. P. (2013). Challenging understandings of inclusive education policy development in Southern Africa through Comparative Reflection. *International Journal of Inclusive Education, 17*(4), 420–434.

Rea-Dickins, P., & Yu, G. (2013). English medium instruction and examining in Zanzibar. In C. Benson & K. Kosonen (Eds.), *Language issues in comparative* education: Inclusive teaching and learning in non-dominant languages and cultures (pp. 189–206). Rotterdam, The Netherlands: Sense Publishers.

Robinson, D. (2017). Effective inclusive teacher education for special educational needs and disabilities: Some more thoughts on the way forward. *Teaching and Teacher Education, 61*, 164–178.

Slee, R. (2011). *The irregular school: Exclusion, schooling and inclusive education.* New York, NY: Taylor & Francis.

UNESCO. (2005). *Guidelines for inclusion: Ensuring access to education for all.* Paris: UNESCO.

UNESCO. (2009). *Policy guidelines on inclusion in education.* Paris: UNESCO.

UNESCO. (2015a). *Incheon declaration, education 2030.* Paris: UNESCO. Retrieved from http://en.unesco.org/world-education-forum2015/incheon-declaration

UNESCO. (2015b). *Embracing diversity: Tool kit for creating inclusive, learning-friendly environments.* Bangkok: UNESCO. Retrieved from http://unesdoc.unesco.org/images/0013/001375/137522e.pdf

UNESCO. (2015c). *Education for all 2015 national review report: United Republic of Tanzania -Zanzibar.* Paris: UNESCO. Retrieved February 20, 2015, from http://unesdoc.unesco.org/images/0023/002314/231428e.pdf

UNESCO. (2015d). *Education for All (EFA) global monitoring report.* Paris: UNESCO. Retrieved March 12, 2016, from http://unesdoc.unesco.org/images/0023/002322/232205e.pdf

UNICEF. (2006). *Assessing child-friendly schools: A guide for programme managers in East Asia and the pacific.* Bangkok: UNICEF. Retrieved from http://www.unicef.org/eapro/Assessing_CFS.pdf

Vuzo, M. (2010). Exclusion through language: A reflection on classroom discourse in Tanzanian secondary schools. *Papers in Education and Development, 29*, 14–36.

Vygotsky, L. (1978). *Mind in society: The development of higher psychological processes.* Cambridge, MA: Harvard University Press.

CHAPTER 4

Inclusive Education Policy and Practice in Ghana: Air Castle or Realistic Goal?

William Nketsia

1 Introduction

Historically, people with disabilities from both Western and Sub-Saharan African countries have been ridiculed, stigmatised, segregated, killed, and abandoned to die (Pritchard, 1963, cited in Kisanji, 1998; Slee, 2013). People with disabilities in Ghana experience a similar fate. They are often locked up, hidden, abused, killed, or excluded from mainstream society and education (Kassah, Kassah, & Agbota, 2012). These maltreatments result from several factors.

Firstly, some Ghanaian cultures demonstrate deep-rooted negative beliefs about the causes of disabilities. Some believe that disabilities are caused by evil or magical powers (juju), sorcery, and witchcraft. In addition, some attribute the causes of disabilities to curses or anger from the gods or deities because of the wrongdoings of family members (Agbenyega, 2008; Naami, 2014; Naami, Hayashi, & Liese, 2012). Consequently, persons with disabilities in Ghanaian communities encounter nerve-racking experiences such as discrimination; stigmatization (Botts & Owusu, 2013); and social, capital, physical, and emotional abuse (Kassah, Kassah, & Agbota, 2012). People with disabilities are excluded from employment and society (Naami, Hayashi, & Liese, 2012). These prejudicial attitudes towards persons with SEN and disabilities pose a serious barrier to social and educational inclusion.

Secondly, the medical model's conception of disability has been quite pervasive in the policies, assessment, and placement procedures for people with disabilities in Ghana (Lamptey, Villeneuve, Minnes, & McColl, 2015). The medical model views disability as being caused entirely or principally by bodily impairment and thus locates intellectual, social, and/or physical deficits within the individual learner. The model views the child as the problem and often ignores social, attitudinal, and environmental barriers to learning (Armstrong, Armstrong, & Spandagou, 2010; Thomas, 2008).

As a result of the two abovementioned factors, educational opportunities in Ghana for children with discernible disabilities, such visual impairments, hearing impairments, and intellectual and developmental disabilities, involve

© KONINKLIJKE BRILL NV, LEIDEN, 2019 | DOI:10.1163/9789004391505_005

predominantly residential or segregated special schools. Those children with non-discernible disabilities, such as partial visual and hearing impairments, behavioural problems, and learning disabilities, attend regular schools, usually without identification or assessment. There has been an increasing shift from the medical perspective to a social perspective of disability. The social model views disabilities as caused by society rather than by individual's impairments. Therefore, it is necessary to focus not on the individuals with impairments but on the societal barriers (i.e. schools) that incapacitate persons with impairments (Armstrong, Armstrong, & Spandagou, 2010).

The exportation of the social model of disability, which has been central to the call for inclusive education, is due to the advocacy of international funding agencies and institutions of global governance. The calls have come in the form of international conventions and declarations, such as UNESCO's 1994 Salamanca Statement, the United Nations' 2006 Convention on the Rights of Persons with Disabilities, and UNESCO's 2015 Incheon Declaration Education 2030 and the 2030 Agenda for Sustainable Development (UNDP, 2015). Article 24 of the United Nation's convention on the Rights of Persons with Disabilities which entered into force in 2008 entreats countries to ensure that persons with disabilities are not excluded from all levels of general education system and that they should ensure an inclusive education system at all.

However, most of the policies and models of inclusive education are developed in different contexts and exported to the developing countries without taking into consideration the broader historical, social, cultural, political contexts of these countries. Armstrong, Armstrong, and Spandagou (2010, p. 126) argue that "reforms systems which equate with 'quick fixes' will be unsuccessful in countries where there are deep-rooted challenges, especially if the reforms do not respectfully consider cultural norms, values and practices". Such exported reforms and policies hardly get fully implemented due to the prevailing structures and conditions of the developing countries. Hence, to successfully implement this noble idea in Sub-Saharan African countries, it is extremely critical for these countries to adopt a critical stance towards inclusive education and develop a contextual understanding of how children with disabilities should be educated (see e.g. Johansson, 2014). Sub-Saharan African countries should identify which basic indigenous principles, practices, and values could serve as foundations on which inclusive education may be implemented (Anthony, 2011; Kisanji, 1998; Pather & Nxumalo, 2012). The onus lies with these countries to draft inclusive education policies that describe their goals and priorities for those excluded from education within those countries. Undoubtedly, the effective implementation of inclusive education in Sub-Saharan African countries will address many deep-rooted challenges.

For instance, Sub-Saharan African countries are culturally, ethnically, socially, and economically diverse. They have the deep-rooted considerable challenges afore discussed such as limited special education services, inadequate funds for education, and discriminatory attitudes towards persons with disabilities due to cultural beliefs. Inclusive education is the logical policy option that has the potential to address all these forms of discriminatory attitudes against children with SEN and disabilities in sub-Saharan African countries. Inclusive policy will ensure the efficiency and cost-effectiveness of the entire education system in sub-Saharan African countries and improve social inclusion and cohesion. Inclusive education will fulfil the right of persons with disabilities to equitable, quality education as well as promote their full human potential, sense of dignity, self-worth, and inclusive society. It will encourage governments to adopt policies to transform education system to offer quality education for all students irrespective of the unique needs, learning styles, abilities, and characteristics of learners. However, it is vital that these international policies are examined and understood in terms of the conditions within each specific country (see e.g. Armstrong, Armstrong, & Spandagou, 2011; UNESCO, 1994, 2006).

2 The Ghanaian Context

After Ghana gained independence, the education policy under the legal framework of the 1961 Education Act recognized education as a fundamental human right for all of Ghana's citizens. Subsequently, the 1992 Constitution of the Republic of Ghana reinforced the right to education by enjoining the state to make required educational facilities available at all levels across the country. The constitution also introduced Free, Compulsory and Universal Basic Education (fCUBE) with the aims of increasing access, increasing participation, improving the capacity to retain and improving the quality of teaching for all school-going children (The Constitution of the Republic of Ghana, 1992). Since then, the right of every Ghanaian child to education has been propagated by various constitutional revisions, such as the Children's Act of 1998 (Act 560) (Republic of Ghana, 1998) and the Persons with Disability Act (Act 715) of 2006 (Republic of Ghana, 2006). These constitutional provisions have made it mandatory for parents and guardians of children with disabilities to send their children to school and for heads of schools to admit them.

Inclusive education and education for all will not be achieved without a clear, unified national policy strategy that includes all learners. The main purpose of most international education policy documents, most importantly the Salamanca Framework for Action, was to influence national education policy and guide governments' actions (UNESCO, 1994, 2009). Following the Salamanca Statement, Ghana enacted relevant inclusive education policies to guide the education of young people with disabilities and SEN within the principles of the right to education, the right to equality of educational opportunity, and the right and obligation to be included in and participate fully in the affairs of society (see e.g. Ministry of Education, 2003, 2012a, 2013, 2015a).

This chapter critically discusses international influences on the local thinking about and development of these important inclusive education policies in Ghana. The chapter highlights some of the key strengths and limitations of the policies and practices. Finally, the chapter addresses the implementation process, the challenges implementation faces, and key recommendations.

3   Inclusive Policy Developments in Ghana

The Education Strategic Plan of 2003–2015 is one of the key Ghanaian inclusive education policy documents developed over the last two decades. Analysis of the policy document indicates that its major focus was the educational ideology of the *integrated education system*. The aim of the policy was to "*integrate all children with non-severe SEN in the mainstream schools by 2015*" (Ministry of Education, 2003, p. 21). It was a Janus-faced policy, which adopted the concept of integration and inclusion interchangeably, as if they meant the same thing. For instance, the two concepts were used in a single sentence, "An *inclusive education system* achieved by 2015, including boys and girls with non-severe SENS *integrated* into mainstream schools" (Ministry of Education, 2003, p. 22). This ambiguity and contradiction was evident in Nketsia, Saloviita, and Gyimah's (2016) recent study in which the majority of teacher educators found it difficult to distinguish between integration and inclusive education, believing that one of the main purposes of inclusive education was to promote integration.

In addition, the strategic plans of 2003–2015 and 2010–2020 conceptualized inclusive education narrowly to promote the inclusion of a specific group of children with non-severe disabilities, the excluded children and the dropouts in regular education. Furthermore, consistent with the individual model of disability and integration, the two strategic plans expected learners with disabilities to fit in special education, special units, mainstream education, or inclusive education. Thus, the plans gave little or no attention to the transformation of the regular education system and the kind of teaching approaches that accommodate all learners.

Inclusive education and integrated education are two different things. The medical model's view of disability undergirds integration and separate special education for children with disabilities. Integration means that students with disabilities and SEN must "get ready" or "be prepared" (Taylor, 1988, p. 223) or "prove their readiness" (Lipsky & Gartner, 1996, p. 765) to move to a regular education environment. In contrast, inclusive education is broadly understood as restructuring the regular education system to make it responsive to the diverse learning needs of all learners in order to achieve social justice and the universal right to equitable, quality education for all (Ainscow, Booth, & Dyson, 2006; Armstrong, Armstrong, & Spandagou, 2010; Slee, 2011).

The current Ghanaian national inclusive education policy has had the strongest alignment with international trends in inclusive education policy. The guiding principles enshrined in the current policy include the following: the right of *all* children to access basic education, and the belief that all children can learn irrespective of differences in age, gender, ethnicity, language, disability, etc. The policy intends to restructure the educational system to adapt structures, systems, and methodologies to meet the needs of all children (Ministry of Education, 2015a). In addition, the current policy has adopted the World Health Organization's (2001) bio-psycho-social model of disability in line with the global shift in the conceptualization of disability. This is essentially a positive departure from the medical view of disability that has for so long dominated policies and practices related to the education of children with disabilities in Ghana. The WHO's bio-psycho-social model conceptualizes disability as an evolving concept that results from the interaction between an individual (with a health condition or impairment) and his/her contextual factors (environmental and personal factors) (WHO, 2001, p. 213). This definition acknowledges the interaction between students and their learning environment and curriculum (see e.g. McGhie-Richmond & Sung, 2013).

Consistent with some of the UNESCO documents (see e.g. UNESCO, 1994, 2005), the current policy has broadly adopted inclusive education as a wider reform to restructure the entire educational system. It seeks to address the diverse learning needs of all students within the Universal Design for Learning (UDL). UDL principles enable teachers to appreciate the variability of learning needs in classrooms and how they can modify the curriculum to meet those needs (Hartmann, 2015). The principles encourage teachers to develop multiple ways of presenting essential concepts so that learners with diverse learning needs can engage in learning, be resourceful, act and demonstrate what they know. The policy furthermore intends to provide equitable access to quality education for all children and promote an inclusive society and values such as participation, friendship, and interaction (Ministry of Education, 2015a).

Contradictorily however, the same policy promotes the inclusion of fragmented categories of children with SEN: gifted and talented children, displaced children, street and nomadic children, orphans, children living in poverty, and children living with HIV/AIDS. Such a broad but fragmented definition of inclusive education seems prevalent in most policy documents from the North and South (see e.g. Johansson, 2014; Pather & Nxumalo, 2012). Armstrong, Armstrong, and Spandagou (2011) have advocated that the fragmentation of "all children" to "different categories" subsequently renders inclusion as a process of "managing" individuals and groups that are perceived as "problems" (p. 32).

Such fragmentations might be grounded in the medical model of disabilities and might encourage the distinction between 'normal' and 'less than normal' pupils (Booth, 1995, p. 99). This categorization might subsequently contribute to a culture of exclusion at both the policy and practice levels of educational provisions, leading to the creation and maintenance of special segregated facilities (Barton, 1997). It could also impede the development of a broader view of inclusion (Ainscow, Booth, & Dyson, 2006). In addition, the categories might attract unwarranted assumptions and oppressions (Thomas, 1997), underestimate groups, or conceal their diversity (Booth, 2005). The adoption of the categories might also influence teachers to locate learning problems within students. But children's learning difficulties in school may arise from other factors such as language, family income, gender, and cultural and ethnic backgrounds (Thomas, 1997). Largely, the categories themselves have little scientific and educational credibility (Armstrong, Armstrong, & Spandagou, 2010, p. 4). It is imperative to characterize learners as being flexible rather than typifying them with immutable categories (Thomas, 1997). In addition, learners must be viewed as having multiple different intelligences and learning styles (Naukkarinen, 2010). These perspectives will enable teachers to shift their focus from the individual students' characteristics to the social context and to encourage the adoption of instructional options and support services for all students.

In addition, the strategic plan of 2003–2015 and the recent Ghanaian inclusive education policy place much emphasis on the screening, identification, diagnosis, referral, and treatment of schoolchildren with disabilities and SEN. These current Ghanaian policies intend to establish assessment centres in all regions and districts for assessment purposes (Ministry of Education, 2015a). Furthermore, the pilot inclusive projects are provided with screening manuals, materials, and teams for the medical and psychological assessment of children as well as the treatment of children for target schools (Ministry of Education, 2013, 2015b). These are examples of practices that are being advanced in the name of inclusive education but have serious exclusionary effects (see e.g. Slee, 2013).

These assessments, screenings, and treatments for subsequent integration are consistent with the international notion medical model of disability. These practices erroneously treat intelligence as a fixed and inheritable feature that can be measured to accurately predict success in school and life (Lipsky & Gartner, 1996). The inevitable labels that result from such assessments have often lacked reliability, validity, and accuracy, with little scientific and educational credibility (Armstrong, Armstrong, & Spandagou, 2010; Slee, 2013). The labels also result in stigmatization, peer rejection, lower self-esteem, lower expectations, and limited opportunities for those labelled (Lipsky & Gartner, 1996). The labels furthermore have been criticized for being costly and dictated by the availability of programmes and space.

In spite of the acceptance of inclusive education ideals and principles, the segregated system of educational provision continues to be dominant at the basic level in Ghana (Ministry of Education, 2013, 2015a, 2015b). Children with specific disabilities such as visual impairments, hearing impairments, and intellectual and developmental disabilities are still educated in special, segregated residential schools and segregated units onsite with mainstream schools (Anthony, 2011; Ministry of Education, 2015a, 2015b). However, due to the lack of expansion of special segregated schools in Ghana, a significant number of children with SEN and disabilities are enrolled in basic mainstream schools across the country (Alhassan, 2014; Ministry of Education, 2015a; Nketsia & Saloviita, 2013; Singal et al., 2015). Kisanji (1998) argued that the inadequate special schools and unofficial integration of learners with SEN in mainstream schools are necessary conditions for the implementation of inclusive education in Sub-Saharan African countries.

Although, separate special education are sometimes recommended for compelling circumstances, such as when the neighbourhood school is unable to meet the needs of the child (see e.g. UNESCO, 1994). However, these special schools promote homogeneous grouping, categorization and labelling, stigmatization, and the social exclusion of children with disabilities and SEN. In addition, the dual system is expensive and does not ensure equal rights and equity in educational provision (Armstrong, Armstrong, & Spandagou, 2010; Florian, 2008). These criticisms have arisen from the growing acknowledgement of the broad continuum of human needs and the inadequacy of separate special education (Armstrong, Armstrong, & Spandagou, 2010). As Stainback and Stainback (1984) succinctly pointed out over three decades ago, all students differ to varying degrees from one another along the same continuums of intellectual, physical, and psychological characteristics. To ensure that the local mainstream schools are substantially improved to address the diverse needs of all learners, some authors have called for the complete abolition of special education (Armstrong, Armstrong, & Spandagou, 2010; Stainback & Stainback, 1984). As Slee (2013, p. 905) indicated 'special schools exist because of the failure of regular schools'. He further admonished that it is problematic to push children into inflexible general educational system and that improvements are required in curriculum, pedagogy and assessment and school design for all students and educators.

Currently, there are over 2000schools that have been practicing inclusive education on a pilot basis in 48 districts across the ten regions of Ghana since the 2003–2004 academic year (Ministry of Education, 2015b). Within each pilot inclusive school, the district staffs, head teachers, and teachers are trained to use appropriate pedagogy, and students are provided with teaching and learning materials, such as assistive devices and braille materials (Ministry of Education, 2013, 2015b). However, the few studies that have evaluated these pilot inclusive schools have found no impact on teachers' attitudes towards inclusion (Agbenyega, 2007; Pekeberg, 2012). The teachers in these inclusive schools have demonstrated negative attitudes towards inclusive education and expressed high levels of concern. Their concerns included large class sizes, inadequate resources and special materials, inappropriate infrastructure, and lack of professional competencies to support students with disabilities in inclusive classes.

The current national policy seeks to provide more relevant professionals such as a physiotherapists, occupational therapists, health workers, and psychologists to support inclusive education (Ministry of Education, 2015a). However, posting all these professionals to every school might not be sustainable considering economic constraints. Some authors also argue that these professionals promote the medical model of thinking about disability (Pather & Nxumalo, 2012) and would add to the restrictiveness of an instructional alternative (Meyen, 1982, cited in Taylor, 1988). It would be more cost-effective and sustainable for these specialists to focus on training and building support teams within schools by equipping school staffs with the required skills and knowledge (see e.g. Pather & Nxumalo, 2012).

Furthermore, the implementation of inclusive education in Ghana involves the following:

a. Integration of students with low vision and blindness in the mainstream schools with the support of itinerant peripatetic teachers,
b. Provision of hostels for pupils with low vision and blindness or the education of students with visual impairment (Blind) within special schools for the Deaf to equip them with the requisite skills to move to mainstream schools and
c. Provision of special units for children with intellectual disability within mainstream schools (Special Education Division, 2011).

These different options represent a special education continuum that allocates learners with disabilities along a range of highly integrated and least restrictive settings to the highly segregated and most restrictive settings (see e.g. Taylor, 1988). The segregated hostels and special schools and units for pupils with low vision and blindness are the most segregated and restrictive placements. This continuum of services is justified on the basis that learners with disabilities will be equipped with additional and appropriate skills to enable them to transition to highly integrated and least restrictive mainstream settings (Special Education Division, 2011; Taylor, 1988). However, Taylor (1988) has identified several shortcomings with this plan.

Taylor (1988) has argued that the existence of a continuum of services presumes that the most restrictive environment is appropriate under certain circumstances and justifies the removal of learners with disabilities from the regular educational environment. In addition, the different placement options in Ghana mean that mainstream schools are incapable of providing the services and supports that learners with disabilities require in order to fully participate. The different options are based on the readiness model, which assumes that learners with disabilities must earn the right, get ready, or be prepared to move to mainstream schools. The different options require professional decision-making to determine the appropriate placement for any individual learner, which diminishes the moral and philosophical justification underpinning inclusive education. Moreover, the continuum restricts the basic rights and liberties of individual learners to participate with learners without disabilities. Furthermore, the allocation of learners with disabilities along the continuum is dependent on the availability of new programmes and spaces and implies that the learners must move as they develop and change. Finally, the different placement options direct attention to physical settings rather than to the services and supports learners need to be included in mainstream schools.

Nonetheless, Ghana has introduced pragmatic national interventions, such as the capitation grant scheme to finance the removal of fees in basic schools; school feeding programmes; the building of schools to reduce distances between home and school; and the distribution of free school uniforms, sandals, scholarships for young girls, and exercise books for needy pupils (Ministry of Education, 2003, 2013, 2015a). These pro-poor and social protection policies have yielded significant achievements in terms of access, gender parity, and equitable basic education for all children (Ministry of Education, 2015a, 2015b). However, inclusive education goes beyond the mere development of new policies and increased physical access to schools. It requires the transformation of regular schools—their curriculum, assessment, and teaching and learning strategies—to address the diverse needs of all learners and to improve quality (Ainscow, Booth, & Dyson, 2006; UNESCO, 1994, 2005; Slee, 2011).

Despite significant developments in policies and access since Salamanca, the reality of inclusive education in Ghana remains a castle in the air. Recent reports by the Ministry of Education estimated that about 25% of schoolchildren with a known disability or SEN, 30% of children with speech disabilities, and 26% of children with physical or intellectual disabilities are out of school. Moreover, 10% of children without disabilities are out of school (Ministry of Education, 2013, 2015a). Furthermore, children with SEN who attend school do so without any support (Ametepee & Anastasiou, 2015). In addition, the enrolment of pupils with SEN in basic mainstream schools fell by 16% in the 2012–2013 academic year, and enrolments in special schools have increased (Ministry of Education, 2013, 2015b). Lastly, the National Education Assessment has consistently revealed that the majority of children in both Primary 3 and Primary 6 fail to achieve minimum competency levels in English and foundational mathematics tests (Ministry of Education, 2014). Consequently, the contextual challenges that exclude many children with disabilities and SEN from meaningful participation in schools in Ghana seems to be significant.

4   Challenges to the Implementation of Inclusive Education in Ghana

Although the current inclusive education policy has adopted the World Health Organization's (2001) bio-psycho-social model of disability, the current analysis indicates that the biomedical perspective of disability still influences practice. A recent study also revealed that the medical perspective of disability is dominant in the SEN courses at the colleges of education (Nketsia & Saloviita, forthcoming). Another challenge is the cultural belief system that attributes the causes of disabilities to curses, witchcraft, punishments from gods, and the possession of evil spirits. A recent study showed that some preservice teachers are predisposed to these cultural beliefs, and their overall attitudes towards inclusive education were barely positive (Nketsia, 2017). The medical model and the cultural beliefs tend to influence teachers to locate the source of learning difficulties within the individual learner rather than within the practical, attitudinal, and environmental factors in school.

Moreover, class sizes in most of the schools exceed the recommended sizes according to the current inclusive education policy (see e.g. Alhassan, 2014; Casely-Hayford, Campbell, Seidu, & Adams, 2013; Singal et al., 2015). The large class sizes affect teachers' attitudes towards inclusive education negatively (Alhassan, 2014) and limit students' engagement and interaction

(Agbenyega, 2008). The large class sizes also encourage the adoption of authoritarian, teacher-centred instructional approaches and the overuse of excessive corporal punishment in order to tame and control students (Alhassan, 2014; Alhassan & Abosi, 2014; Casely-Hayford et al., 2013; Ministry of Education, 2015b). As a result, Ghanaian teachers treat children on the same intellectual basis and fail to acknowledge diversity among learners (Agbenyega, 2008). This practice makes most children with disabilities and SEN feel isolated and bored in classrooms due to their inability to understand the lessons taught (Alhassan, 2014; Singal et al., 2015).

Furthermore, the implementation of inclusive education in Ghana is challenged by inadequate facilities, textbooks, syllabi, teachers, assistive devices, exercise books, and teaching and learning materials (Agbenyega, 2007, 2008; Casely-Hayford et al., 2013; Ministry of Education, 2015b; Nketsia & Saloviita, 2013; Singal et al., 2015). The schools also have inaccessible buildings and lack sidewalks, ramps, elevators, and kerb cuts (Ministry of Education, 2015b; Naami, 2014). Moreover, special education and inclusive education receive very little financial support (Ametepee & Anastasiou, 2015). As a result, schooling and transportation costs are high, there is no curriculum support, and attendance and access for students with disabilities is poor (Ministry of Education, 2015b; Singal et al., 2015).

Again, mainstream classroom teachers demonstrate limited knowledge of and competence in inclusive instructional strategies that address the needs of pupils with SEN (Alhassan, 2014; Alhassan & Abosi, 2014; Agbenyega, 2007, 2008; Casely-Hayford et al., 2013; Nketsia & Saloviita, 2013; Singal et al., 2015). This limitation has been attributed to the lack of emphasis on inclusive and child-centred instructional approaches in teacher-training programmes (Alhassan, 2014; Nketsia, Saloviita, & Gyimah, 2016).

Additionally, the centralized, prescriptive curriculum in Ghana traditionally has not been designed for diversity and is unresponsive to the needs of minority groups and students with disabilities and SEN. This curriculum also reinforces the dominance of teacher-centred teaching approaches in Ghanaian classrooms (see e.g. Loreman, 2007; Price, 2015). The examination-oriented nature of the centralized national curriculum in Ghana makes the situation even worse. The emphasis on children's marks and grades contradicts the principle of inclusion because it disengages students with disabilities and SEN and can have negative effects on teachers' attitudes towards inclusion (Forlin, 2010; Gaad, 2004). Also, the centralised curriculum and emphasis on grades influence teachers to adopt authoritarian teaching methods (Tafa, 2004) and view their performance as delivering curricula rather than responding to the needs of learners through interactive pedagogy (Edwards & Protheroe, 2003).

A study by Gaad (2004) in the United Arab Emirates revealed that teachers opposed the idea of teaching children with intellectual disabilities in their classrooms because the children's failure in examinations would be blamed on the teachers. This is in line with Slee (2013) argument that high stakes testing makes schools selective about which students they will enrol, making schools shy of difference. The following are key recommendations to ensure successful implementation of inclusive education in Ghana.

5 Key Recommendations

Taken together, the key issues highlighted in this chapter suggest that inclusive policy, inclusive practice, and teacher education curricula must adopt a more social model perspective on disability. Inclusive education must be viewed as a human rights approach to social justice and democratic societies. These steps will ensure the successful removal of barriers within local schools and increase participation for all children in the curricula, cultures, and communities.

Moreover, the findings reverberate the burning need for reforms in teacher education programmes. The colleges of education must be restructured to effectively equip pre-service teachers with the requisite knowledge, skills, and attitudes to effectively respond to individual differences among children. Several studies from non-Western countries have established the usefulness of inclusive and learner-centred pedagogies in supporting inclusion and dealing with difference in the classroom (see e.g. Forlin & Sin, 2010). Some of the learner-centred approaches found to be effective for including pupils with disabilities and SEN in large mainstream classrooms in Ghana and other Southern African countries include group work; mixed ability groupings; peer-assisted, differentiated learning strategies; and cooperative learning approaches (Alhassan, 2014; Singal et al., 2015).

Pre- and in-service teacher education programmes have the responsibility to identify and equip teachers with these local evidenced-based child-centred approaches. This will ensure that teachers have the confidence and professional responsibilities to make the centralized curriculum in Ghana accessible and increase expectations and learning progression for students with disabilities. The Universal Design for Learning principle adopted in the current inclusive education policy must form an integral part of the initial education curriculum. This strategy will equip teachers with the skills and knowledge to appreciate the variability of learners' needs and make significant changes in their lesson plans to optimally include all and respond to learners with SEN (see e.g. Hartmann, 2015; McGhie-Richmond & Sung, 2013).

There are other innovative strategies for improving teachers' knowledge about inclusive teaching approaches and transforming teachers' attitudes towards disability. These strategies include the adoption of planned pupil-focused SEN tasks to enable teachers to engage in a direct teaching experience with a student with SEN under the supervision of an experienced SEN coordinator. The colleges of education must include action-research initiatives in school to try the effectiveness of certain instructional approaches.

Moreover, genuine political commitment is required to ensure small and manageable class sizes and accessible learning environments (i.e. schools buildings) for all students. The government must provide the adequate resources, instructional materials, basic infrastructure, and support systems needed for inclusive education. Essentially, more empirical studies on the pilot inclusive projects are required to determine if the projects are sustainable, appropriate, and contextually relevant. The effective inclusive approaches, attitudes, knowledge, and skills in the pilot inclusive schools must be determined and promulgated across schools. They could also form part of the initial teacher training curriculum.

In addition, the current examination-oriented culture must be realigned to support greater inclusion. Assessing the quality of an education system must not be confined to academic achievement; it must include both cognitive and emotional development as well as the promotion of the values, attitudes, and social and functional skills of responsible citizens (see e.g. Kisanji, 1998). Substantial reforms are required in the Ghanaian education system in order to acknowledge the needs of diverse children and accept, welcome, and value different educational outcomes.

6   Conclusion

The closer examination of the Ghanaian national policies and legislations has substantiated Slee (2013, p. 895) proposition that "the human rights charters and national legislation around the world will not in and of themselves rid us of exclusion" and that some of the practices that are being advanced in the name of inclusive education have serious exclusionary effects. For instance, the fragmentation of "all children" to "different categories" in the definition of inclusive education; the provision of screening manuals and the emphasis on the medical and psychological screening, diagnosis, referral, and treatment of schoolchildren with disabilities in the pilot inclusive projects; and the continuum of placement options. The expected impacts of these practices in pilot inclusive schools are that more students will be caught up in the diagnostic net, teachers can name different categories of disabilities and recite their 'aetiologies and symptomologies'. Teachers will then believe that they are not qualified to teach these children and therefore rush for special help or call for more resources (see e.g. Slee, 2013, p. 905).

Moreover, the placement options defeat the essence of inclusive education, which requires reforming the educational system rather than requiring individual learners to change in order to participate in regular education. It is therefore important to recommend that Ghana and other Sub-Saharan African countries adopt decisive steps to gradually avoid over-reliance on a continuum of special segregated services and create a unified educational system for all learners. Slee (2013) admonished that more efforts should focus on how to build the capacity of schools to address diversity in schools. The unconditional right of all learners to attend mainstream schools will promote the cost-effectiveness of inclusive education and kindle strong political will to ensure the full provision of services and supports necessary for all learners to participate fully in local regular education.

Further, this chapter clearly reinforces the widely held view of the enormous influence of international declarations, statements, and conventions on the policies of Sub-Saharan African countries. However, the current inclusive policy development process in Ghana has been interactive and participatory in nature, with much consideration of the broader local context. The process has gained supports, commitments, and contributions from local political, administrative, and traditional leaders as well as many stakeholders in public institutions, civil society, the private sector, and local communities. This phenomenon has assured some level of agreement and sense of ownership, and it has made the policy quite the vox populi of the Ghanaian people. Pather and Nxumalo (2012) argued that such alliances inspire passion and creativity and change the view that inclusive education is only for learners with disabilities and SEN and that only special education specialists and professionals should advocate it.

Finally, the policy implementation has also redefined the role of special education and key actors such as parents, communities, families, councils for persons with disability, etc. For instance, special educators could adopt the role of resource teachers and instructional teams that develop instructional materials, technological capabilities, and effective methods of teaching all children in mainstream classrooms. Another key strength has been the shift in the conceptualization of disability away from the medical model to that of an interaction between an individual with impairments and his/her contextual factors. Yet another positive step has been the introduction of strategies for monitoring and evaluating implementation in order to ensure quality and sustainability.

References

Agbenyega, J. S. (2007). Examining teachers' concerns and attitudes to inclusive education in Ghana. *International Journal of Whole Schooling, 3*(1), 41–56.

Agbenyega, J. S. (2008). Developing the understanding of the influence of school place on students' identity, pedagogy and learning, visually. *International Journal of Whole Schooling, 4*(2), 52–66.

Ainscow, M., Booth, T., & Dyson, A. (2006). *Improving schools, developing inclusion.* London: Routledge.

Alhassan, A. K., & Abosi, O. C. (2014). Teacher effectiveness in adapting instruction to the needs of pupils with learning difficulties in regular primary schools in Ghana. *Sage Open, 4*(1), 215824401351892. doi:10.1177/2158244013518929

Alhassan, A. M. (2014). Implementation of inclusive education in Ghanaian primary schools: A look at teachers` attitudes. *American Journal of Educational Research, 2*(3), 142–148. doi:10.12691/education-2-3-5

Ametepee, L. K., & Anastasiou, D. (2015). Special and inclusive education in Ghana: Status and progress, challenges and implication. *International Journal of Educational Development, 41*, 143–152.

Anthony, J. (2011). Conceptualising disability in Ghana: Implications for EFA and inclusive education. *International Journal of Inclusive Education, 15*(10), 1073–1086. doi:10.1080/13603116.2011.555062

Armstrong, A. C., Armstrong, D., & Spandagou, I. (2010). *Inclusive education: International policy and practice.* London: Sage Publications.

Armstrong, A. C., Armstrong, D., & Spandagou, I. (2011). Inclusion: By choice or by chance? *International Journal of Inclusive Education, 15*(1), 29–39. Retrieved from http://dx.doi.org/10.1080/13603116.2010.496192

Barton, L. (1997). Inclusive education: Romantic, subversive or realistic? *International Journal of Inclusive Education, 1*(3), 231–242.

Booth, T. (1995). Mapping inclusion and exclusion: Concepts for all? In C. Clark, A. Dyson, & A. Millard (Eds.), *Towards inclusive schools?* London: David Fulton.

Booth, T. (2005). Keeping the future alive: Putting inclusive values into action. *FORUM, 47*(2–3), 151–158.

Botts, B. H., & Owusu, N. A. (2013). The state of inclusive education in Ghana, West Africa. *Preventing School Failure: Alternative Education for Children and Youth, 57*(3), 135–143. doi:10.1080/1045988X.2013.798776

Casely-Hayford, L., Campbell, S., Seidu, A., & Adams, R. (2013, September 10–12). *The quality and inclusivity of basic education across Ghana's three northern regions: A look at learning effectiveness and efficiency in post 2015.* UKFIET International Conference on Education and Development – Education & Development Post 2015, Reflecting, Reviewing, Re-visioning, Oxford.

Edwards, A., & Protheroe, L. (2003). Learning to see in classrooms. *British Educational Research Journal, 29*(2), 227–242.

Florian, L. (2008). Special or inclusive education: Future trends. *British Journal of Special Education, 35*(4), 202–208.

Forlin, C. (2010). Future direction for teacher education for inclusion. In C. Forlin (Ed.), *Teacher education for inclusion: Changing paradigms and innovative approaches* (pp. 246–252). Abingdon: Routledge.

Forlin, C., & Sin, K. (2010). Developing support for inclusion: A professional learning approach for teachers in Hong Kong. *International Journal of Whole Schooling, 6*(1), 7–26.

Gaad, E. (2004). Cross-cultural perspectives on the effect of cultural attitudes towards inclusion for children with intellectual disabilities. *International Journal of Inclusive Education, 8*(3), 311–328. doi:10.1080/1360311042000194645

Hartmann, E. (2015). Universal Design for Learning (UDL) and learners with severe support needs. *International Journal of Whole Schooling, 11*(1), 54–67.

Johansson, S. T. (2014). A critical and contextual approach to inclusive education: Perspectives from an Indian context. *International Journal of Inclusive Education, 18*(12), 1219–1236. doi:10.1080/13603116.2014.885594

Kassah, A. K., Kassah, B. L. L., & Agbota, T. K. (2012). Abuse of disabled children in Ghana. *Disability and Society, 27*(5), 689–701. doi:10.1080/09687599.2012.673079

Kisanji, J. (1998). The march towards inclusive education in non-western countries: Retracting the steps. *International Journal of Inclusive Education, 2*(1), 55–72.

Lamptey, D., Villeneuve, M., Minnes, P., & McColl, M. A. (2015). Republic of Ghana's policy on inclusive education and definitions of disability. *Journal of Policy and Practice in Intellectual Disabilities, 12*(2), 108–111.

Lipsky, D. K., & Gartner, A. (1996). Inclusion, school restructuring, and the remaking of American society. *Harvard Educational Review, 66*(4), 762–796.

Loreman, T. (2007). Seven pillars of support for inclusive education: Moving from "why?" to "how?" *International Journal of Whole Schooling, 3*(2), 22–38.

McGhie-Richmond, D., & Sung, A. N. (2013). Applying universal design for learning to instructional planning. *International Journal of Whole Schooling, 9*(1), 43–57.

Ministry of Education. (2003). *Education Strategic Plan (ESP) 2003–2015: Policies, targets and strategies* (Vol. 1). Accra: Ministry of Education.

Ministry of Education. (2012a). *Education Strategic Plan (ESP) 2010–2020: Policies, strategies, delivery, finance* (Vol. 1). Accra: Ministry of Education.

Ministry of Education. (2012b). *Education sector performance report*. Accra: Ministry of Education, Republic of Ghana.

Ministry of Education. (2013). *Education sector performance report*. Accra: Ministry of Education, Republic of Ghana.

Ministry of Education. (2014). *Ghana 2013 National Education Assessment: Technical report*. Accra: Ghana Education Service, National Education Assessment Unit.

Ministry of Education. (2015a). *Inclusive education policy.* Accra: Ministry of Education, Republic of Ghana.

Ministry of Education. (2015b). *Education sector performance report.* Accra: Ministry of Education, Republic of Ghana.

Naami, A. (2014). Breaking the barriers: Ghanaians' perspectives about the social model. *Disability, CBR and Inclusive Development, 25*(1), 21–39.

Naami, A., & Hayashi, R. (2012). Perceptions about disability among Ghanaian university students. *Journal of Social Work in Disability & Rehabilitation, 11*(2), 100–111. doi:10.1080/1536710X.2012.677616

Nash, T., & Norwich, B. (2010). The initial training of teachers to teach children with special educational needs: A national survey of english post graduate certificate of education programmes. *Teaching and Teacher Education, 26,* 1471–1480.

Naukkarinen, A. (2010). From discrete to transformed? Developing inclusive primary school teacher education in a Finnish teacher education department. *Journal of Research in Special Educational Needs, 10*(1), 185–196.

Nketsia, W. (2017). A cross-sectional study of pre-service teachers' conceptualization of disability and attitudes towards inclusive education. *International Journal of Research Studies in Education, 6*(3), 53–68.

Nketsia, W., & Saloviita, T. (2013). Pre-service teachers' views on inclusive education in Ghana. *Journal of Education for Teaching, 39*(4), 429–441. doi:10.1080/02607476.2013. 797291

Nketsia, W., & Saloviita, T. (forthcoming). *Teacher educators and trainees' perspective on teacher training special education course.*

Nketsia, W., Saloviita, T., & Gyimah, E. K. (2016). Teacher educators' views on inclusive education and teacher preparation in Ghana. *International Journal of Whole Schooling, 12*(2), 1–18.

Pather, S., & Nxumalo, C. P. (2012). Challenging understandings of inclusive education policy development in Southern Africa through comparative reflection. *International Journal of Inclusive Education, 17*(4), 420–434. doi:10.1080/13603116. 2011.651821

Pekeberg, I. M. B. (2012). *Inclusive education in Ghana: An analysis of policies and the practices in one mainstream school and one inclusive school in the greater Accra* (Master thesis). University of Oslo, Oslo.

Price, D. (2015). Pedagogies for inclusion of students with disabilities in a national curriculum: A central human capabilities approach. *Journal of Educational Enquiry, 14*(2), 18–32.

Republic of Ghana. (1998). *Children's act* (Act 560). Accra: Republic of Ghana.

Republic of Ghana. (2006, June 23). *Persons with disability act* (Act 715). Accra: Republic of Ghana.

Singal, N., Salifu, E. M., Iddrisu, K., Casely-Hayford, L., & Lundebye, H. (2015). The impact of education in shaping lives: Reflections of young people with disabilities in Ghana. *International Journal of Inclusive Education, 19*(9), 908–925.

Slee, R. (2011). *The irregular school: Exclusion, schooling and inclusive education.* Abingdon: Routledge.

Slee, R. (2013). How do we make inclusive education happen, when exclusion is a political predisposition? *International Journal of Inclusive Education, 17*(8), 895–907. doi:10.1080/13603116.2011.602534

Special Education Division. (2011). *Initiatives in implementation of inclusive education descriptive models.* Accra: Ghana Education Service.

Stainback, W., & Stainback, S. (1984). A rational for the merger of special and regular education. *Exceptional Children, 51*(2), 102–111.

Tafa, E. M. (2004). Teacher socialization: A critical qualitative analysis of the teaching methods of seven new teachers in Botswana junior secondary schools. *International Journal of Educational Development, 24*, 757–758.

Taylor, S. (1988). Caught in the continuum: A critical analysis of the principle of least restrictive environment. *Journal of the Association for Persons with Severe Handicaps, 13*, 41–53.

The Constitution of the Republic of Ghana. (1992). Retrieved December 29, 2015, from http://www.ghanaweb.com/GhanaHomePage/republic/constitution.php

Thomas, C. (2008). Disability: Getting it "right". *Journal of Medical Ethics, 34*, 1–17.

Thomas, G. (1997). Inclusive schools for an inclusive society. *British Journal of Special Education, 24*(3), 103–107.

UNDP. (2015). *Sustainable development goals.* Retrieved October 17, 2016, from http://www.undp.org/content/undp/en/home/librarypage/corporate/sustainable-development-goals-booklet.html

UNESCO. (1994). *The Salamanca statement and framework for action on special needs education.* Paris: The United Nations Educational, Scientific and Cultural Organization (UNESCO).

UNESCO. (2005). *Guidelines for inclusion: Ensuring access to education for all.* Paris: The United Nations Educational, Scientific and Cultural Organization (UNESCO).

United Nations. (2006). *Convention on the rights of persons with disabilities and optional protocol.* New York, NY: United Nations. Retrieved December 29, 2015, from http://www.un.org/disabilities/default.asp?id=150

World Health Organisation (WHO). (2001). *International classification of functioning, disability and health.* Geneva: World Health Organisation.

World Health Organization and World Bank. (2011). *World report on disability.* Geneva: World Health Organization and World Bank.

CHAPTER 5

In Search of an Inclusive Pedagogy in South Africa

Sigamoney Manicka Naicker and Sindiswa Stofile

1 Introduction

Inclusive Education is a necessity in the developing world, particularly in countries where there is a rich poor divide such as South Africa. Given the history of oppression and marginalization of the majority of the population in apartheid South Africa, schools have emancipatory and transformative roles particularly in relation to disability, race, socioeconomic background and gender. All the White papers in South Africa emphasized the value and importance of schools as transformative agents since South Africa is one of the most unequal societies in the world. The number of people that earn very low salaries is staggering and many children grow up in these households. Bowles and Gintis (1976) mentioned that schools reproduce the status quo and besides a few exceptions in South Africa, that is the reality. Globalization and Neo-liberalism has entrenched the inequality and one vehicle to transform a future society is undoubtedly education. Former Finance Minister of South Africa, Pravin Gordhan delivered a keynote address at the University of Johannesburg recently sketching a new global economy in which millions of people who were able, willing, educated and trained will never find a job. This, said Gordhan, was one of the downsides of globalization, which had divided the world into winners and losers and which has created an instability and unpredictability that has forced "sheer misery" on millions across the globe who march barefooted from one country to another while at the same time becoming victims of xenophobia and other forms of attack (Daily Maverick, 2017). The crime and violence that is inflicted on society is outrageous and much of this is a result of children dropping out of the schooling system. The state will save millions of rands if more children finish their schooling. In fact the attrition rate is close to 50% in some provinces in South Africa and the accumulation of such large numbers leaving the schooling system is taking its toll on the crime statistics and the general stability of the society almost two decades after the advent of a democratic government. This chapter will focus on the need for South Africa to search for an inclusive pedagogy through very real changes in the structure and practice of education. We have to embrace diversity and provide an education that takes seriously the context of our learners.

© KONINKLIJKE BRILL NV, LEIDEN, 2019 | DOI:10.1163/9789004391505_006

The South African education system is not looking at the total well-being of children but at advancing a performative culture. As a result several children are failing in the early years and become part of the attrition rate. Many of the children who emerge from poor backgrounds experience challenges with staying in school, perform poorly in reading and mathematics and also experience severe trauma particularly those who live in high crime areas. So the major theme of this chapter is why is success so elusive for so many children in South Africa?

This chapter will discuss: (i) what is a performative culture? (ii) the socio-economic portrait of the second richest province in South Africa, the Western Cape, and its possible implications for teaching and learning,(iii) What does research tell us about children who are traumatised? (iv) that majority of children do not have their basic needs met and therefore success In schooling is so elusive, (iv) the search for an inclusive pedagogy (v) some recommendations for the South African education system to move towards an inclusive pedagogy

2 What Is the Performance Culture?

The lens of bureaucrats and people in government are focused on the performance of the system. Nothing else matters besides the Grade 12 results and children's performance in Grade 3, 6 and 9. Many of these bureaucrats do not challenge the system when large numbers of children are not placed in facilities that require specialized support, for example, autism. These personnel are rewarded for efforts associated with the performance culture. They are less likely to pay attention to children who experience barriers. Social justice and equity issues become less important since the key aspect of the system in terms of recognition and reward are for Grade 3, 6 and 9 results and Grade 12 results. This is not a recent phenomenon. Supranational organizations such as the United Nations, the European Union, and the Organization for African Unity, the International Monetary Fund and the World Bank play a crucial role in the process of education policy formulation and implementation across diverse socio-political contexts. Ball (2012) discusses the cosmopolitan nature of education policy reforms by exploring the ways in which global politics and policies are reciprocally related and have an immense impact on national reform efforts. These global agencies are key players in shaping the 'context of influence' (Berkhout & Wielemans, 1999, p. 417) against which national education policy agendas are conceptualized, negotiated and enacted, while it is frequently the case that they articulate contradictory responses to globalization (Vongalis-Macrow, 2005). As such, they confound the process of education policy formulation and implementation (Berkhout & Wielemans, 1999).

3   The Social and Economic Portrait of the Western Cape

Economists Samuel Bowles and Herbert Gintis (1976) in their treatise School-ing in Capitalist America: Education Reforms and Contradictions of Economic Life have documented sufficiently how schools reproduce the status quo. Fam-ilies play a crucial role in the rearing and development of children. Schools experience major difficulty in rupturing the status quo.

The following discussion highlights the importance of families in early lit-eracy development. Parents and other significant adults support children's language learning through conversation, encouraging imaginative play, and by reading stories, singing nursery rhymes and buying books. They support their children's learning by talking about how they are doing at school, encouraging them to join the library and entertaining high aspirations for children to pro-ceed to higher education. When this crucial home literacy support is not there, as is the case of many South Africans, children start school at a disadvantage and it is more difficult for children to catch up. Those with poor literacy are more likely to be unskilled, in and out of work and vulnerable to structural changes in the workplace (Bird, 2007).

The socio-economic conditions in families determine to a large extent the quality of learning environment at home. The Western Cape is the second rich-est province and it is important to look at its socio economic portrait as well as the implications for teaching and learning. According to the Provincial Eco-nomic Review and Outlook research in 2007, 25.5% of people in the Western Cape are unemployed. A further analysis of the data indicates the following:

- Between the ages of 15 and 24, 49.1% are unemployed.
- Between the ages of 25 and 34, 23.7% are unemployed.
- Between the ages of 35 and 44, 18.1% are unemployed.
- Between the ages of 45 and 54, 13.1% are unemployed.

A large percentage of younger parents who are likely to have young children are unemployed. These homes have limited educational resources and lack a print culture, and early literacy is minimal. This implies few books, little inter-est in school work and a lack of a reading and oral language culture.

Another alarming characteristic of the socio-economic portrait relates to education levels. There is a link between education levels of parents and learners' performance. According to the PERO (2007), in the Western Cape:

- 1.5% of people have no education at all.
- 24.2% have education at Grades 0–8 level.
- 22.7% have education at Grades 9 to 11, NTC 1 and 11 level.
- 11% have diploma or certificates.
- 6.8% have degrees.

Fleisch (2008) indicates that one of the single strongest predictions of under-achievement is parents' education attainment. According to Fleisch, studies consistently find strong positive associations between the duration of school careers and children's success of schools. It is no surprise that for those learn-ers currently at school in the Western Cape, only 37% of learners at Grade 3 level achieve grade-appropriate literacy and numeracy levels. At Grade 6 level, numeracy performance drops to 15%, and literacy performance to 35%. These statistics are alarming if we consider that the education sector receives 38.1% of the total provincial budget (Human Capital Development Strategy, 2007, p. 10).

Stannard and Huxford (2007) found in the British National Literacy Strategy that most children who fail at school came from poor homes with a poor learn-ing environment from the early years onward. Stanndard and Huxford (2007) find that the majority of children in the UK who underachieve do so due to their prior experience at home; they appear less active, reluctant to learn and fail to benefit from school. Failing children in the classrooms use different strategies for bringing the world under control. They learn that school is often unpredictable and brings risk of failure. Their lives are less certain and more insecure, so they opt for strategies that keep them out of trouble. Stanndard and Huxford (2007) further find that these children found it more predict-able and thus safer to fail than to attempt to succeed. These children tend to say 'Yes' when the teacher asks: 'Do you understand?'; they wave their hands when the teacher asks the class a question because they guess they are less likely to be asked; if they are asked, they repeat the question and hesitate until the teacher, impatient to see them succeed, gives them sufficient clues or tells them the answer; they will choose to wait in a queue at the teacher's desk for help with spelling to avoid facing the challenge of the task, and so on. These children are not passive but they have put a different construction on schools and learning – one that frequently manifests itself noticeably and early in failure to learn reading and writing. Many children in the Western Cape are traumatised by gun violence and other forms of violence.

4 What Does Research Tell us about Children Who Are Traumatised?

Whilst there is a major concern about children who cannot cope with literacy and numeracy, little is done about children who are traumatised by poverty. These children are unable to focus and learn as a result of the crime and poverty. Some schools in the Western Cape are surrounded by gangs and there is disruption of schooling on a regular basis.

IN SEARCH OF AN INCLUSIVE PEDAGOGY IN SOUTH AFRICA

One is forced to ask the question, can the large numbers of children in the Western Cape focus on teaching and learning in their classroom? Jim Paterson (2017) provides some useful insights into this topic. Troy is smart, but disrupts classes all day and is in detention at least once a week. He's regularly the topic of disparaging talk among teachers and administrators, and is well-known by the attendance office for missing school. He mutters "I don't care" in response to the lectures he frequently receives.Ellie sits behind him in math, and in this class and throughout her day teachers get very little work or response. Juan, on the other hand, who is required to sit in the front, just can't stop talking and disrupting class.

These three middle school students will often get extra attention in school, but won't succeed because the real reason for their behavior isn't addressed: trauma. This is the experience of many children in the Western Cape.

From severe bullying, emotional abuse, or death of a parent at home to a classmate's suicide or a school shooting, we now know trauma diminishes the performance and good behavior of students – and limits their health and happiness as adults. It is harder, however, to see how the many proposed approaches to combat it can be implemented consistently during a busy school day, but experts say professional development is a good start.

According to a federal Trauma and Justice Strategic Initiative in the United States, "trauma results from an event, series of events, or set of circumstances that is experienced by an individual as physically or emotionally harmful or threatening and that has lasting adverse effects on the individual's functioning and physical, social, emotional, or spiritual well-being" (Steinberg et al., 2014). It generally overwhelms an individual's ability to cope, the report says, and it often ignites "fight, flight, or freeze" impulses, and produces a sense of fear, vulnerability, and helplessness, and later can cause people to act anti-socially or irrationally.

The National Child Traumatic Stress Network (NCTSN) (Steinberg et al., 2014) in the United States reports that one-out-of-every-four children attending school has been exposed to a traumatic event that can hamper their learning – and affect school and class culture since they will likely be disruptive or need extra attention. The organization reports (Steinberg et al., 2014). that research shows these students typically have diminished reading skills, lower GPA's, higher rates of absenteeism, suspension and expulsion, and are much more likely to drop out.

Schools that have implemented trauma-informed policies, meanwhile, they find they get positive results. There are examples in San Francisco, Seattle, New Orleans, New York and, perhaps most famously, in Wala Wala, Washington, where improved school data has been reviewed and supported. Research also suggests that the trauma-informed schools are making gains, and that professional development should be combined with a school-wide policy shift to make new approaches work.

A recent issue of the journal School Mental Health provides extensive research about trauma in schools and concludes in an article about the effectiveness of trauma-informed practices that "when school systems approach students through a trauma lens, they are better equipped to provide the educational and social/emotional supports necessary to help students reach their potential". It says to accomplish that they "must support more intensive professional development" (2016, pp. 1–6).

Patterson (2017) indicates that Sandra Chafouleas, a professor of educational psychology at University of Connecticut (2017) has reviewed successful approaches to professional development for staff, noting that it starts with teaching staff members more about trauma. She says along with understanding trauma better, teachers should be able to identify it and know how to establish a "safe environment" and develop good relationships, often by better understanding student "triggers" that come from their difficult experience.

She says that informational part of a staff development program should help unlock another key element – building a consensus. NCTSN has a detailed *list of strategies* for teachers that can be part of the training, but experts note that it is critical to begin with a structure for broadening the approach to the whole school.

Chafouleas says an effective program requires clear planning with input from all stakeholders and specific expected outcomes, along with a well-defined system for delivery of the program, ongoing coaching and support for the staff, and a monitoring system which uses accurate, useful data.

According the Mental Health Journal that has trauma in schools as a special focus, school counselors are trained to help students deal with trauma, but often have large caseloads – from 300–1,000 students – which means all staff should be trained to help identify students who have suffered trauma (2016, pp. 1–6). It also means schools may need outside resources for training and working with students. Some experts say schools might inform the staff about social work practices and others have developed models for schools that include community resources.

There is voluminous amounts of research on trauma-informed schools and ideas for staff development, much of which can be found with organizations such as the National Childhood Traumatic Stress Network in the United States with its specific resources for educators, along with Trauma and Learning Policy Initiative and the federal government's center for trauma-informed care in the United States. The state of Wisconsin has also put together an extensive list of resources for its educators.

IN SEARCH OF AN INCLUSIVE PEDAGOGY IN SOUTH AFRICA   93

Here are five things educators can do to help trauma victims that might not seen immediately evident.

– Anticipate problems with students by noticing cues. This requires that educators note what triggers certain behavior and are sensitive to them. It's also helpful if such information is communicated to others.
– Give them choices. Often traumatic events involve chaos or loss of control, so you can help children feel safe by providing them with options and more opportunity to control their environment – when appropriate.
– Set clear, firm limits for inappropriate behavior and develop *logical* – rather than punitive – consequences. So, rather than responding immediately to an event (often angrily), gather information and help student understand the affect of their action, what they could have done differently and what the fair consequences are.
– Understand that children cope by re-enacting trauma through play or through their interactions with others. Watch for it with other students and resist their efforts to draw you into a negative repetition of the trauma, for instance, replaying abusive situations.

Paterson (2017) argues that we need to provide provide one-on-one support. One person designated to connect regularly with a traumatized student can have a major impact. Some experts recommend a "2 x 10" approach, where a teacher spends two minutes every day one-on-one with a difficult student without distractions for 10 school days. "You don't need an agenda, just the willingness to talk and listen about something that interests the student", says Pamela Canter, CEO of Turnaround for Children, which was founded to support students in New York after the 9–11 attacks and now advises schools on trauma solutions. Arguably the number of children affected by trauma is limited compared to those that do that have their basic needs addressed.

5 The Majority of South African Children's Basic Needs Are Not Being Satisfied and Therefore Success Is So Elusive?

For South Africa to achieve improved Grade 3, 6 and 9 results as well as Grade 12 and impact significantly on the throughput rate, much attention should be paid to the holistic development of children. Children from poorer homes need a safety net and Maslows hierarchy of needs is a good framework for education policy makers. Whilst a discussion of all Maslows needs are mentioned in this chapter they are not discussed in considerable detail. A few are discussed to illustrate the possibilities and these highlight the shortcomings of the South African education system.

Despite the attempts to advance inclusion in South Africa, there has been a notable increase in the number of withdrawals from public ordinary schools of learners labelled as having special educational needs and these learners have been placed in special schools or remain in public ordinary schools without appropriate support (Department of Education, 2015a). This practice has been heavily criticised, contested and challenged by the Equal Education Law Centre because of the belief that there is a lack of political will in this country to address the needs of all learners. If this belief is legitimate, the question is: Which needs are not being satisfied?

6 Which Needs Are Not Satisfied?

Maslow's (1943) theory of human motivation is a very useful framework for explaining and understanding needs that motivate effective learning. Maslow believes that certain conditions are prerequisites for the basic need satisfactions. These conditions include:

> freedom to speak, freedom to do what one wishes so long as no harm is done to others, freedom to express one's self, freedom to investigate and seek for information, freedom to defend one's self, justice, fairness, honesty, orderliness in the group. (Maslow, 1943, p. 383)

The five stage model (Maslow, 1943) has been expanded to include cognitive and aesthetic needs as well as transcendence needs (Maslow, 1970). Needs are categorised into a hierarchy, in which certain needs must be met before others (Maslow, 1943). In other words, lower needs must be satisfied before higher-order needs can be reached. If these needs are denied, the desire to fulfil such needs will become stronger. When learners are concerned about certain basic needs, their behaviour will focus on meeting those needs than learning and achievement Burleson and Thoron (2014). Figure 5.1 presents the hierarchy of different needs.

Failure to satisfy physiological needs of children in South Africa is evident in different research reports. This status quo persists despite the implementation of the National School Nutrition Programme (NSNP, 2004) that provides meals to learners in lower quintiles from poor communities. In developing this programme, the Department of Education acknowledges the need to satisfy learners' hunger needs. NSNP is intended to provide a well-balanced diet and nutritious meals to learners, with the hope of improving school attendance and learners' concentration and performance (Barnett, 2014).

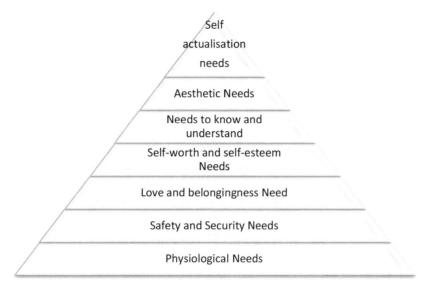

FIGURE 5.1   Maslow's hierarchy of needs (from Burleson & Thoron, 2014, reprinted with permission)

Rendall-Mkosi, Wenhold, and Sibanda (2013) reported that some school going age children showed signs of nutritional problems in the form of stunting (18%), wasting (4%) and overweight (6%), and up to 20% of households experienced food insecurity). There are also reported cases of informal settlement children who still go to school without food (Maarman, 2009; Stofile, Linden, & Maarman, 2011). Maarman asserts that this deprivation hinders learners' capabilities because these learners have neither the freedom nor the capacity to choose the lives they place value on. Stofile, Linden, and Maarman (2011) suggest that hunger and poor nutrition, in particular, cause physical and psychological conditions that contribute to learners' inability to participate fully and effectively in the education services provided. Hunger disempowers all involved in the educating process (learners, teachers, parents or guardians), and constrains the quality of teaching. To emphasise the importance of satisfying hunger needs, Maslow (1943) claimed that:

> For the man who is extremely and dangerously hungry, no other interests exist but food. He dreams food, he remembers the food, he thinks about food, he emotes only about food, he perceives only food and he wants only food. (p. 373)

Although NSNP is implemented in South Africa, why do we still have reports that show that hunger needs are not satisfied? Wildeman in Barnett (2014, p. 94) claimed that the inconsistent funding has compromised the delivery of the school feeding programmes at schools, a situation that has compromised learners' access to quality education, and to the development of their capabilities. Whilst the South African government must be complemented for running such a wonderful programme, many of these children do not eat at home. For many of them, their only meals are the ones they receive in school.

In terms of safety and security needs, Maslow (1970) regards these as essential for a person's well-being. What threats to their physical, mental, or emotional security do learners experience in schools? Safety and security in South African schools is a huge challenge. There are many examples of the extreme consequences of school violence (van der Westhuizen & Maree, 2009), such as axe-killing by schoolmates (Mqota, 2007); fatal stabbing (Etheridge, 2016; Khoza, 2015; as well as the occurrence of shooting and assaults on the school grounds (Khoza, 2015). The National School Violence Study (NSVS) undertaken by the Centre for Justice and Crime Prevention (CJCP) in 2012 reveals that 22.2% of high school learners were found to have been threatened with violence or had been the victim of an assault, robbery and/or sexual assault at the school in the previous year. The threats sometimes are so prevalent that many learners feel that their survival may depend on carrying a weapon for protection in their neighbourhoods and schools (DeCarlo, 2012).

These statistics show that children's safety and security needs are not effectively addressed. Children are placed in a state of anxiety and feelings that harm will physically, mentally, or emotionally befall them at any time. This has devastating effects for learners, teachers and parents, and results in many of the behavioural, social and educational problems that confront the nation, including school drop-out. Is the safety and security problem being addressed in South African schools? It is worth acknowledging that attempts have been made by the Department of Education to create safe schools through the implementation of the National School Safety Framework (NSSF). This framework serves as a tool for Provincial and District Officials responsible for school safety, principals, Senior Management Team Members, SGB members, teachers and learners to identify and manage risk and threats of violence in and around schools (Department of Basic Education, 2015b). This framework is very impressive, but it appears as if it is not properly implemented by schools and closely monitored by designated officials in districts.

The Equal Education Law Centre Annual Report of 2016 (EELC, 2016) reveals that many schools still lack the basic infrastructure that facilitates quality learning. This report claims that children from low-income families are being forced to learn in unsafe dilapidated structures that have broken windows, appalling sanitation facilities, unsafe drinking water; and no electricity or security. These hostile and unsafe learning environments can threaten learners' well-being and prevent them from participating in educational activities and gaining access to knowledge. Although the Regulations Relating to Minimum Uniform Norms and Standards for Public School infrastructure has been published in 2013, a process towards the improvement of infrastructure in the worst-off schools is very slow (EELC, 2016). Unsafe and insecure learning environments could also include environments where learners feel bullied or disliked by other learners or teachers, fear of being ridiculed, taking risks, asking questions, sharing their thoughts and answering questions. In addition, Burleson and Thoron (2014) posit that learners view safety through a predictable world and if the routine has not been established, they are likely to feel anxious and unsafe. These authors link anxiety to underperformance.

The need for love and belonging is one of the basic needs in a child's life, but it is often overlooked in schools. A sense of belonging is generally regarded as one of the most important basic needs of human beings. Goodenow (1993, p. 80) claims that a sense of belonging at school reflects 'the extent to which students feel personally accepted, respected, included, and supported by others in the school social environment'. Many theorists suggest that the feeling that you belong is important in seeing value in life. Learners who experience a sense of belonging in educational environments are more motivated, more engaged in school and classroom activities, and are more dedicated to school (Osterman, 2000). Failure to satisfy the need of belonging can cause the experience of negative emotions such as feelings of social isolation, anxiety and depression.

In 2016, South Africa experienced an uproar from learners and parents who experienced racial discrimination, severe abuse and neglect in multiple schools. In a number of cases teachers and principals were found to have exposed pupils to dehumanising and racist treatment. This practice leads to feelings of rejection, insecurity and being outcasts among the affected learners. In different political platforms in South Africa citizens claimed that the formerly white schools have opened their doors but they have not changed their attitudes towards other racial groups. The 2016 news reports were dominated by Black South African girls' protests over hair policies that banned natural African hairstyles because they are deemed untidy. At the centre of these protests, were claims that Black girls' hair is a central component of their identity and culture and for decades South African schools have robbed them of it. A Cape Town writer Will-Ed Zungu (2017), in his article, argued that "schools not only make black people hate their hair at an emotional level but at an institutional level". These reports construct South African schools as geographical spaces that breed racism and perpetuate white supremacy in more furtive ways. This, however, contravenes Section 9(3) of the South African

Constitution which prevents school governing bodies from making rules that unfairly discriminate against learners because of their race, ethnicity gender, beliefs or culture. Learners need to feel accepted and that they belong to their schools, their communities and their country. In addition, learners should feel psychologically and emotionally safe within their learning environment (Burleson & Thoron, 2017).

7 The Search for an Inclusive Pedagogy

Has South Africa made a genuine attempt to move towards an inclusive pedagogy? Giroux (2003, p. 11) understands pedagogy as "a moral and political practice crucial to the production of capacities and skills necessary for students to both shape and participate in social life" If close to 50% of our learners are dropping out of the schooling system and if large numbers of children are not learning to read and pass numeracy then we are not involved in a moral and political practice that makes our learners independent and self-sufficient to lead a complete life. How has our planning changed in order to move towards an inclusive pedagogy? What significant shifts have there been in the system to bring about a change to an inclusive education system?

South Africa has advanced an inclusive education agenda but if one analyses the interventions much is yet to be achieved. A section was added to the CAPS curriculum on diversity. Thus the notion of barriers to learning does not form the basis of the CAPS curriculum which means the CAPS curriculum does not take inclusive education seriously. The fact that South African Sign Language was not written by curriculum experts during the CAPS process suggests that there were two processes in curriculum development, one for special schools and one for mainstream schools. Another experience of many children with special needs is that they are not accepted within the mainstream since principals fear they will reduce the pass rate. Schools are rewarded for a 100% pass rate. The curriculum in any country creates the platform for inclusion. With every subject there are barriers to learning as well in the schooling system. These barriers should be addressed if we want to develop an inclusive education system.

It seems like the search for an inclusive pedagogy has been hijacked by the need to pursue the performative culture. Those students, whose performative worth has been perceived as being incompatible with dominant effectiveness indicators, have been negatively positioned and relegated to the margins of education. These developments have resulted in the creation of a 'performative' culture of public schooling (Ball, 2004; Ball & Olmedo, 2013) that promotes mono-dimensional conceptualizations of teaching and learning gauged

IN SEARCH OF AN INCLUSIVE PEDAGOGY IN SOUTH AFRICA

against standardized tests, performance indicators and league table rankings. (Anastasia Liasidou & Loizos Symeou, 2016) Anastasia and Loizos sums up the problem. It is all about human worth and who is the ideal and non-ideal person for the capitalist market as well as the apparent credibility of the system. Unfortunately there is a relationship between poverty and disability and what has happened in view of this performative culture social justice and equity which was one of main thrusts of the South Africa's transformation has fallen aside.

Given South Africa's past one would have expected that inclusion and an inclusive pedagogy become the central feature of South African education planning. Unfortunately, the planning occurred outside the framework of inclusion. Two very good examples mentioned above include the implementation of the Curriculum and Assessment Statements (CAPs). This curriculum is a body of knowledge cannot be introduced to all learners in the same way. Oral language acquisition and vocabulary development should be based on the level the learner is at. Some children come to school with low levels of vocabulary and oral language. That presents with a major problem in terms of learning to read. Many of these children don't learn to read by the age of 8 which means they may never learn to read unless there is a reading recovery programme which is nonexistent in our schools. These are the learners that leave school early. There has to be a differentiation between learners. We cannot introduce the curriculum in the same way for children of parents who earn R80 000 a month and those than earn R8000 a month. Schools can play a major role in alleviating social inequalities and minimizing the achievement gap between privileged and disadvantaged groups of students on the basis of their ethnic, racial, linguistic, social class and so forth characteristics (Bass & Gerstl-Pepin, 2011; DCSF, 2009).As mentioned earlier, Giroux (2003, p. 11) understands pedagogy as "a moral and political practice crucial to the production of capacities and skills necessary for students to both shape and participate in social life". Our focus should not be on the performative culture but rather the attempt to create level playing fields in the classrooms of our country. The sad situation is that South Africans have been captured by neoliberalism and Giroux is incisive when he points out points to the fact that under the siege of neoliberal discourse, issues regarding schooling and social justice, persistent poverty, inadequate healthcare, racial apartheid in the inner cities, and the growing inequalities between the rich and the poor have been either removed from the inventory of public discourse and public policy or factored into talk show spectacles that highlight private woes bearing little relationship either to public life or to potential remedies that demand collective action (Giroux, 2003, p. 8).

The moral and political practice of establishing an inclusive space in every educational endeavor should be at the top of the agenda. In all our classrooms and schools the question should be asked, how can we include every child? The alternative is what is happening now when half the schooling population leaves the education system before they leave Grade 12. The South African school curriculum should be learner centred and educationists should not see the learner audience as homogenous. Teaching methodology and content should reflect and understanding and entrenchment of barriers to learning. This should be a vital component of every teacher's training.

8 Recommendations in Pursuance of an Inclusive Pedagogy

There several ways in which the system can change with a view to pursuing an inclusive pedagogy. The basis for change has to be underpinned by a value for all children. If there is a genuine desire to support all children then then the pedagogy employed in schools could be regarded as moral and fair. The system can benefit from the following changes:

- A safety net for learners in the poorest schools should be a priority with a holistic focus not restricted to reading and writing.
- CAPS should be introduced differently to children whose parents earn R8000 per month and R80 0000 per month.
- Focus on all the needs of children. Make schools inclusive. That should be the point of departure.
- Before looking at performance, South Africa should look at healthy schools. Developing healthy schools will automatically develop healthy schools.
- Middle class education is different from working class education. We need to acknowledge this and understand this. We cannot impose middle class working models on working class schools. So far it has proved not to work.
- Planning should be inclusive. This includes learner transport, learner and teacher support material, curriculum development, early childhood education, examinations and assessment. We should discourage have special education units in department and make them responsible for the transformation.
- There should be a shift from Grade 3, 6 and 9 as well as Grade 12 to the well-being of all learners in all schools.
- The Foundation Phase should be a three year phase with different goals for different children depending on their overall development.
- Maslow's needs should be taken seriously and act as the basis for child development in our schools.

IN SEARCH OF AN INCLUSIVE PEDAGOGY IN SOUTH AFRICA

- Building blocks for all children should be built into the Foundation Phase.
- There should be one learner transport system.
- There should be one system for building new schools.
- There should be one system of education for all learners.
- Every attempt should be made to ensure every child learns to read.
- Begin a reading recovery programme similar to that in New Zealand and other parts of the world.
- We should move away from a performance culture to a culture of respect for each child irrespective of their background.
- Systemic tests should only be introduced after systems are put into place that gives every child an equal chance in school

9   Conclusion

South Africa should shift from moving towards a performative culture to one that makes healthy schools a point of departure. The imposition of performance on schools has created a stress culture which deviates from a real education agenda. Children who are poor and those who suffer from trauma must have their basic needs met. Many of these children with unmet needs in the formative years drop out of school or fail repeatedly. Often the trauma and unmet needs are the problem. This is one way of addressing the high drop-out rate and the large number of children who fail to read. There has to be a greater focus on children who need support as a result of poverty and trauma. Teaching for tests and lack of respect for the challenges of diversity will strangle what little is left of the learning culture. Learning can only flourish in circumstances where the holistic child becomes the focus of learning and teaching. Too many children in South Africa sit on the margins because of poverty and historical factors related to apartheid. They need to be brought to the centre.

References

Ball, S. J. (2012). *Global education inc.: New policy networks and neo-liberal imaginary.* London: Routledge.
Ball, S. J., & Olmedo, A. (2013). Care of the self, resistance and subjectivity under neoliberal governmentalities. *Critical Studies in Education, 54*(1), 85–96. doi:10.1080/17508487.2013.740678

Barnett, E. M. (2014). *A capability analysis of education policies in quintile 1 schools in the Frances Baard district of the Northern Cape province* (Doctoral thesis). University of the Western Cape, Cape Town.

Berkhout, S., & Wielemans, W. (1999). Toward understanding education policy: An integrative approach. *Educational Policy, 13*, 402–420. doi:10.1177/0895904899013003004

Bowles, S., & Gintis, H. (1976). *Schooling in capitalist America: Educational reform and the contradictions of economic life.* New York, NY: Routledge.

Burleson, S. E., & Thoron, A. C. (2014). *Maslow's hierarchy of needs and its relation to learning a n d achievement.* Gainesville: Department of Agricultural Education and Communication.

Burton, P., & Leoschut, L. (2012). *School violence in South Africa: Results of the 2012 national school violence study.* Cape Town: Centre for Justice and Crime Prevention.

DeCarlo, A. (2012). A developmental explanatory model of maladaptive aggression dispositions in urban African American adolescents. *Sage Open, 2*, 1–13. Retrieved from http://www.sgo.sagepub.com

Department of Basic Education. (2015a). *Report on the implementation of education White paper 6 on inclusive education: An overview for the period 2013–2015.* Pretoria: Government Printer.

Department of Education. (2015b). *National safety schools framework.* Pretoria: Government Printers.

Equal Education Law Centre. (2016). *Equal education law centre annual report.* Cape Town: Equal Education Law Centre.

Giroux, H. A. (1992). *Border crossings: Cultural workers and the politics of education.* New York, NY: Routledge.

Giroux, H. A. (2003). Public pedagogy and the politics of resistance: Notes on a critical theory of educational struggle. *Educational Philosophy and Theory, 35*(1), 5–16.

Giroux, H. A. (2011). *Education and the crisis of public values.* New York, NY: Peter Lang.

Goodenow, C. (1993). The psychological sense of school membership among adolescents: Scale development and educational correlates. *Psychology in the Schools, 30*, 70–90.

Khoza, A. (2015, November 4). Grade 9 pupil stabbed to death outside the school gate. *News 24.*

Liasidou, A. (2016). Inclusive education and critical pedagogy at the intersections of disability, race, gender and class. *Journal for Critical Education Policy Studies, 10*(1), 168–184.

Liasidou, A., & Symeou, L. (2016). Neoliberal versus social justice reforms in education policy and practice: Discourses, politics and disability rights in education. *Critical Studies in Education, 59*(2), 149–166. doi:10.1080/17508487.2016.1186102

Maarman, R. (2009). Manifestations of capabilities poverty with learners attending informal settlement schools. *South African Journal of Education, 29*(3), 317–331.

Maslow, A. H. (1943). A theory of human motivation. *Psychological Review, 50*(4), 370–396. doi:10.1037/h0054346

Maslow, A. H. (1968). *Toward a psychology of being.* New York, NY: Van Nostrand Reinhold Company.

Maslow, A. H. (1970). *Motivation and personality.* New York, NY: Longman.

Mqota, V. (2007, June 3). No learning in a climate of fear. *Sunday Argus*, p. 25.

Osterman, K. F. (2000). Students' need for belonging in the school community. *Review of Educational Research, 70*, 323–367.

Our Schools Are the Breeding Ground of Racism in South Africa. (2017). *Huffington post South Africa.* Retrieved June 3, 2017, from http://www.huffingtonpost.co.za/will-zungu/our-schools-are-the-breeding-ground-of-racism-in-south-africa_a_21702956/

Patterson, J. (2017). *Why your school should be implementing trauma-informed practices in education world.* Retrieved from https://www.educationworld.com/why-your-school-should-be-implementing-trauma-informed-practices

School Mental Health. (2016, March). Trauma-informed schools: Introduction to the special issue. *School Mental Health, 8*(1), 1–6.

Steinberg, A. M., Pynoos, R. S., Briggs, E. C., Gerrity, E. T., Layne, C. M., Vivrette, R. L., Beyerlein, B., & Fairbank, J. A. (2014). The National child traumatic stress network core data set: Emerging findings, future directions, and implications for theory, research, practice, and policy. *Psychological Trauma: Theory, Research, Practice, and Policy, 6*(Suppl. 1), S50–S57.

Stofile, S., Linden, N., & Maarman, R. (2011). Teacher-reported poverty effects on education participation in a South African district. *Journal of Psychology in Africa, 21*(4), 603–605.

Thamm, M. (2017, May 23). Gordhan: Glorification of globalisation has masked its considerable downsides. *Daily Maverick.*

Van der Westhuizen, C. N., & Maree, J. G. (2009). The scope of violence in a number of Gauteng school. *Acta Criminologica, 22*(3), 43–62.

CHAPTER 6

Special and Inclusive Education Policy and Practice in Kenya, 1963 to 2016: The Journey

Martin Mwongela Kavua

1 Introduction

Inclusive education (IE) has been articulated in policy, for instance, the Education For All (EFA) resolutions in Jomtien and Dakar, as well as the Salamanca statement (UNESCO, 1990, 1994, 2000) and global policy guidelines on inclusive education (UNESCO, 2009). In these documents, UNESCO calls on countries to draft National policies on inclusive education tailored for their requirements. In line with this, Kenya endeavours to create policies in education aligned with obligations set out in the conventions she has signed, and her context. Moreover, policies signal the direction in local education to the global agenda informed by the millennium development goals (UNESCO, 2009; Crossley, 2012) and now the sustainable development goals (SDG). In one study which the author was involved in, policy emerged as a significant factor in determining practices within school settings (Kavua, 2014), revealing importance even at the micro level. Since an inclusive society is the most appropriate setting for all persons including those with disabilities, Inclusive Education (IE) should be the most appropriate for attaining such society (Jenkins & Barr, 2006; Ministry of Education Science and Technology, 2009).

This chapter explores definitions for inclusive education, critically discusses legislation and policy governing practice in special and inclusive education in Kenya since independence. The author draws from his experience in Newham Borough, London, England, where he was involved in a study on inclusive education for learners with hearing Impairment (HI) to inform part of the discussion.

2 Defining Inclusive Education

Agreeing on what constitutes an inclusive education or setting appears to be elusive. Despite the fact that IE has been accepted and supported by most governments in policy and sometimes in practice, its definition remains

© KONINKLIJKE BRILL NV, LEIDEN, 2019 | DOI:10.1163/9789004391505_007

problematic and varied. In the United Kingdom (UK), the National Association of Schoolmasters Union of Women Teachers (NASUWT) (2008) and Powers (2002), acknowledge that definitions for IE are complex, varied and highly contextualized. Moreover, the House of Commons' education and skills committee expressed difficulties establishing the definition of IE by the UK government (House of Commons, 2006). Countries differ in their definitions and practice of inclusive education. What some may refer to as IE may be seen as integration by others. A case in point is the concept specially provisioned schools in Newham Borough in England. In my experience, there exists significant resemblance between inclusive education practices in Newham and integrated programmes in Kenya. In the borough, a school is specially equipped with resources to cater for learners with a specific disability, for instance, hearing impairment. The learners access the curriculum in both a special, and/or regular class as their abilities in specific subjects allow (Kavua, 2014). While some see these as inclusive settings, they bear significant resemblance to integrated programmes in Kenya, therefore, their inclusiveness might be questioned especially those from backgrounds similar to Kenya.

Powers (2002) points out that it is confusing whether inclusion refers to a goal (e.g. ending 'educational segregation' through closing all special schools), a state (e.g., all children educated in mainstream classrooms), a process (e.g., of increasing participation for children with special needs), a means to an end (e.g., mainstream education as a way to better academic outcomes for all), or a value system (e.g., one concerned with the rights of all marginalized groups) (p. 230). Ainscow (2005) appears to borrow heavily from Powers (2002) in his proposed four elements to guide a definition for inclusive education. He suggests the following for consideration as elements of inclusive education:

1. A process of always seeking better ways to respond to diversity
2. Identification and removal of all barriers to learning
3. Physical presence and participation of all learners including those with special needs and disabilities.
4. Emphasis on groups deemed as at risk to exclusion. Categories of learners perceived to be most at risk should be carefully monitored to ensure their presence, participation and achievement in the education system.

UNESCO (2009) views IE as the process of strengthening systems of education and improving schools in order to serve all learners and establish a system of education that is open to all while addressing all learners' needs (UNESCO, 1994, 2005, 2007, 2009). Therefore, IE can be defined as a system of education that addresses the needs of all learners regardless of diversity. In Kenya, MOEST (2009, 2010) defines inclusive education as a process of addressing and responding to the diversity of needs of all learners through increased participation in learning, cultures and reduction of exclusion in education. It involves changes and modifications in content, approaches, structures, and strategies with a vision which takes care of all learners.

The philosophy of IE has not gone without opposition. The British Deaf Association (BDA) at first voiced resistance to the placement of learners with hearing impairment (HI) in mainstream schools especially when not placed as a group in the same school to relate as members of the Deaf community (BDA, 1996 in Jarvis et al., 2003). Moreover, research suggests that communication for learners with HI in schools traditionally for hearing learners is potentially problematic, as it leads to cultural segregation (Cawthon, 2001; Jarvis et al., 2003; Armstrong et al., 2010). Apprehensions about placement of learners with different special needs and disabilities in the same class with typically developing peers is common among opponents of IE. I believe that since most people agree that IE is the most appropriate option for all learners, details of how different stakeholders define it should form part of the wider discussions around IE, towards deeper understanding, and a possible common definition.

3 Educational Legislation, Policy and Practice towards Inclusive Education in Kenya

This section discusses post-independence educational policies and legislation which have influenced special and inclusive education practice in Kenya. Legislation and policies in Kenya are established through commissions, working committees and parliament (Randiki, 2002; MOEST, 2009). The direction taken by an education system is guided by the route map created through legislation and policy. They are an important ingredients of an effective education system because they facilitate access to services and ensure equity. Policies empower parents to have their children attend any school of their choice, have a say in what and how their children learn, identify infringement of children rights and discrimination, as well as have a framework for seeking redress where aggrieved, with support from the law. However, since they are sometimes politically and culturally driven, they can be used to exclude sections of society (Jenkins & Barr, 2006). For instance, in Kenya, the Fraser report (1909) and Phelps/Stokes commission (1924) recommended racially segregated education, which was implemented until independence.

As the country gained independence from the British in 1963, there was need to focus on education to suit the requirements of the country and empower citizens to take up positions left behind by returning British citizens

(Ntarangwi, 2003). Two committees were set up in 1964: the Ngala Mwendwa and the Ominde commissions. Prominence was given to rehabilitation and integration of learners with SNE, as well as introduction of special education components to teacher training to support integration. Integration was later restated by the National Committee on Educational Objectives and Policies (1976). It did not involve environmental adjustments to cater for learners' needs (Sifuna & Otiende, 1994). Emphasis was laid on four main disability areas i.e. hearing impairment, visual impairment, mental handicaps, and physical handicaps, hence sidelining other learners with SNE. Introduction of special education as a subject in regular teacher training was not implemented to date. Moreover, there was lack of structured early identification and intervention structures and skilled personnel to carry out the assessments (MOEST, 2009).

As a consequence of the issues mentioned above, the National Committee on Educational Objectives and Policies (Republic of Kenya [RoK], 1976) recommended early intervention and assessment of children with special needs, creation of public awareness on causes of disabilities to promote prevention, and research to determine the nature and extend of handicaps for provision of Special Needs Education (SNE). Consequently, Educational Assessment and Resource Centres (EARC) were established in 1984 (MOEST, 2009). Moreover, pre-school programmes were established in special schools to mitigate for late intervention and limited access to education (RoK, 1976).

The 7-4-2-3 system was deemed unsuitable for the country's needs in the 1980's because it prepared graduates for white color jobs which were getting scarce (Sifuna & Otiende, 1994). The system was changed from 7-4-2-3 where students spent 7 years in primary school, 4 in O' level and 2 in A' level secondary education in 1985, while university education took a minimum of 3 years. The 8-4-4 system was introduced where students take 8 years in primary, 4 years in secondary and a minimum of 4 years in university education respectively. Technical subjects were introduced with the aim of developing self-reliance and self-employment (Chang'ach, 2013). The subjects included home science, art and music among others (RoK, 1981), which could be said to be appropriate for learners with cognitive challenges since they are practical and not only academic. Major challenges have been faced in practice leading to withdrawal of some subjects from the curriculum (Ambaa, 2013). For instance, the proposed formative evaluation was proven impractical from the initial stages resulting in purely summative evaluation. Over time, various factors have combined to necessitate the currently ongoing education reforms. These include challenges in proper quality assurance in education as proposed by the Kamunge report (RoK, 1988). Simiyu (2001) and Ambaa (2013) cite lack of infrastructure and resources to implement the 8-4-4 curriculum as a major challenge.

The Totally Integrated Quality Education and Training Commission (TIQET) (RoK, 1999) noted lack SNE policy in the country as a concern, and recommended that one be drafted. A draft SNE policy was created a decade later in 2009 (MOEST, 2009). The policy provides guidelines on inclusive education, provision of a barrier free environment, and addresses barriers to inclusion. The TIQET report was pro-inclusive education because it proposed improved early intervention of SNE, improved curriculum accessibility, equity, relevance and quality with special attention to gender sensitivity, persons with SNE and disabilities (RoK, 1999; Randiki, 2002). In consideration of international conventions that the government of Kenya has signed so far, for instance the Salamanca statement (UNESCO, 1994), and the World Conferences on Education For All (EFA) (UNESCO, 1990, 2000), there is need to have an inclusive education policy as proposed by TIQET. Although some developments can be witnessed today, much remains to be done in relation to the suggestions of TIQET.

In the last decade and a half, focus seems to have shifted to parliamentary legislation as opposed to appointed commissions on matters related to guiding progress in special and inclusive education. The Children's Act (RoK, 2001) harmonized all existing laws and policies on children into one document. It aims at improving the wellbeing of ALL children irrespective of diversity. The act reiterates the rights of a child to free, compulsory basic education that meets the needs of all learners. Basically, the following rights are protected. The right to: Name and nationality; education; parental care; religious education; healthcare; protection from armed conflict and child labour; protection from abuse and harmful cultural practices like female genital mutilation and early marriages among others (RoK, 2010). Later, it was realized that there was need for further legislation to secure the rights of persons with disabilities.

Thereafter, the Persons with Disabilities Act was in 2003. The act provides a comprehensive legal framework which outlaws all forms of discriminative treatment of persons with special needs and disabilities in all areas including education. It provides for adaptation of infrastructural, socio-economic and environmental facilities to ensure a conducive environment for persons with special needs and disabilities. To operationalize it, the act establishes the National Council for Persons with Disabilities (NCPWD) to oversee implementation of other recommendations within the Act. The Council is mandated to enforce the conditions of a least restrictive environment on public and private institutions including schools, as well as public service vehicles. This could ensure educational and social inclusion for persons with disabilities.

In 2002, the National Rainbow Coalition (NARC) – a political alliance, made a campaign pledge to offer Free Primary Education (FPE) if elected, which they implemented in 2003. Under FPE, school levies were abolished, learning materials provided, and direct financial support for schools given among others. As a result, enrolment rates soared. Consequently, schools were faced with the challenges of overcrowding, inadequate resources, and overworked teachers which led to low education quality (RoK, 2003a or 2003b; MOEST, 2005). However, FPE does not cover boarding fees and other mandatory requirements which learners with special needs and disabilities require for education in special schools. Over time, enrolment has dropped, and so have quality standards. Additional challenges include embezzlement of FPE funds, and mismanagement. The MOEST is in the process of taking away the responsibility of school heads to buy books and locally in order to have them purchased from a central office at the headquarters in Nairobi.

Sessional Paper No. 1 of 2005 recognizes the paradigm shift from special to inclusive education especially for learners with SNE and disabilities. However, special schools and units are still recognized in the paper as important in provision of education for some learners. The sessional paper addresses the logistical aspects of providing inclusive education such as access, funding, training, research, promotion of barrier free environment and staffing at all levels.

The National Policy Framework on Education (2012) aligns education to the constitution of Kenya 2010 (discussed below) and Kenya vision 2030 (Government of Kenya, 2007). Vision 2030 is Kenya's master plan for development by the year 2030. Education is set as a component under the social pillar of the vision. In the policy framework, enhancement of accessibility and equity in educational provision at all levels is identified as a key component of education towards achieving vision 2030 (Government of Kenya, 2007). The constitution of Kenya (RoK, 2010) asserts that any treaty or convention ratified by Kenya forms part of domestic law. Article 54 of the constitution provides for inclusion of persons with disabilities in education as a right. Discrimination on any basis is prohibited in article 27 (4) (5) (RoK, 2010), and the basic education act (MOEST, 2013). Concealing a person with disabilities is a crime under section 45 of the constitution. The constitution declares Kenyan Sign Language (KSL) an official language, thus empowering Deaf people. Article 7(3) (b) provides for appropriate communication to be provided for persons with sensory impairments, including provision of sign language interpreters during television newscasts. Chapter 4 forms an elaborate bill of rights. On education, article 53(b), (d) and (e) protect the right to free and compulsory basic education; and protection from all abuse and exploitation among others.

Although article 53 states the rights of children, rights for children with disabilities are emphasized in part 3 of article 54 of the constitution which emphasizes specific rights for persons with disabilities. The right "to access educational institutions and facilities for persons with disabilities that are integrated into society to the extent compatible with the interests of the person" is reiterated. Access is extended to public transport; communication and access to information; and access to materials and devices to overcome the effects of disability. The constitution further strengthens the NCPWD by incorporating within it the provisions of the persons with disabilities act (2003).

The Basic Education Act (number 14) (2013) currently governs education in Kenya. Apart from spelling out the functions of national and county education boards, the act gives direction on components of free and compulsory education. Part IV of the act states that every child has a right to free and compulsory basic education. It defines basic education as pre-primary, primary and secondary education. Admission and tuition fees are abolished in primary schools under the act. However, it should be noted that some public schools still charge tuition fees and other levies, which in itself presents a conflict between policy and practice. Part IV of the act leaves out inclusive schools when it lists institutions to be established by the cabinet secretary of education to provide education for learners with special needs and disabilities. It gives substantial attention to integrated programmes, bringing to question the government's commitment to entrench inclusive education in the country's education system.

The Basic Education Act (Republic of Kenya, 2013) lists categories of learners with Special Needs in Education (SNE) including learners with Autistic spectrum disorders, children under especially difficult circumstances, and various sensory and cognitive impairments among others. This is useful in planning for service provision and training of specialists. It commits the government to provide free primary and secondary education for them, provide adequate personnel for SNE, as well as infrastructure development. Section 43 gives the secretary of education authority to regulate the establishment and management of institutions that provide services for learners with special needs in education. This empowers the secretary to ensure provision of inclusive education for learners with special needs in all institutions as deemed possible. Since the act provides for the amount of time to be spend in any specific level of education, it may minimize exclusion through forced repetition of classes especially for learners with intellectual challenges.

In 2012, a new government was elected to power riding on the promise of introducing digital device assisted learning in the country. The Kenya Institute of Curriculum Development (KICD) has already developed interactive digital content for class 1 to 3 (Ministry of Information Communication and Technology, 2015). Despite litigation related challenges, the Digital Literacy Programme (DLP) has been piloted and devices delivered to the country. The programme was launched in late September 2016. Distribution of devices is on-going with every school expected to have them before January 2017 when they will be used for learning in all public primary schools starting in class 1 (Nation Media Group, 30/09/2016). It is hoped that the DLP will succeed as planned.

4   Challenges Faced When Implementing Educational Policy in Kenya

Insufficient personnel, limited skills, poor infrastructure and equipment for learners with SNE affect policy implementation and inclusive education (Nthia, 2009). Moreover, the Kenya National Human Rights Commission (KNHRC) (2014) highlights the need for learners with special needs in education to be supported by other professionals alongside teachers in order to be supported to fully participate in education. These professionals include sign language interpreters; teacher aides; Braille transcribers; speech therapists; audiologists and educational psychologists among others. Such professionals are scarce in Kenya as previously discussed. This challenge can be addressed through sharing personnel among institutions as I witnessed in England where speech therapists serve several schools. A similar practice can be adopted for Kenya as well.

Learners with special needs and disabilities in education require adaptations in the environment in order to enhance access the curriculum like other learners (Hiuhu, 2007). This takes material resources to achieve. Furthermore, assistive and adaptive devices are costly. To address this, the persons with disabilities act (RoK, 2003a or 2003b), provides for zero rating taxes for devices and vehicles for persons with disabilities (PWDs) to increase access. It is possible to overcome resource related limitations by using specially provisioned schools for inclusive education within a certain geographical region. Newham Borough in London utilizes this kind of strategy. A school is provided with resources and personnel to cater for learners with a certain disability within inclusive education.

Cultural beliefs and practices influence how society views causes of disabilities, treats persons with disabilities, and provides solutions for them (Ravindran & Myers, 2011). Riddell and Watson (2003) stress that "The socially dominant culture shapes the way in which disability and impairment are viewed, and has contributed to the oppression of disabled people" (p. 1). In Kenya, these believes have not favored persons with disabilities, since terms used to describe them have been derogatory, while their treatment has extended to infanticide in some cultures. Culture includes religious and social norms (Frederickson & Cline, 2002). Main religions present persons with disabilities as incomplete and in need of healing. E.g. the deaf shall hear if prayed for a common belief, while others are encouraged to treat persons with disabilities with pity and mercy so as to acquire God's goodness. All these take away the person with disability's right to be treated as an equal human being. Cultural practices and attitude have long been unfair to persons with disabilities. While they should be changed, this cannot be done without offering alternatives, therefore, education should offer culture sensitive solutions (Ravindran & Myers, 2011). Inclusive education offers this alternative education for accommodating all learners for an inclusive society.

The responsibility of education is shared between the government and communities. Government pays salaries, provides learning resources and policy while communities usually construct school infrastructure in collaboration with government. In Kenya, communities have established institutions through the cost sharing initiative recommended by the Kamunge report (RoK, 1988). Requirement by government for communities to financially contribute towards basic education has led to exclusion of low income sections of society. It is important to note that establishment of SNE in Kenya has its origins in charity. Churches established most institutions for SNE in Kenya as philanthropic activities, as a result, parents and communities may not feel obliged to educate children with disabilities (Randiki, 2002). Creation of awareness is necessary in order to improve the situation (MOEST, 2009). The World Health Organization (WHO) (2011) acknowledges that parents of children with disabilities may find it more difficult to pay school fees and levies since they have to cater for higher costs of healthcare, diet and dedicate time to services related to special needs and disabilities.

Support services to habilitate, rehabilitate and support learners with SNE make significant contributions to improved livelihoods (WHO, 2011). However, many are either not locally available, or expensive. A case in point is occupational therapy, which is so scarce in Kenya that the ratio of therapists to the population is nearly 1:10,000 (WHO, 2011). Besides, most support service providers work under other government ministries outside education, which presents challenge in coordination of service provision in education.

Corruption has been a major challenge in Kenya. Transparency International (TI) identifies gross mismanagement, unaccountability, and secrecy in running projects in the sector as major challenges (TI, 2010). Some officers have been found guilty of corrupt dealings in education (idid.). Martini (2012) identifies corruption as a major barrier to accessing resources and services.

SPECIAL AND INCLUSIVE EDUCATION POLICY AND PRACTICE IN KENYA   113

Corruption diverts money that would have been used for programmes for persons with disabilities to other irrelevant (mis)uses (TI, 2010).

In order to achieve IE for all, the government should pay for SNE for learners with special needs and disabilities in order to reduce the burden of parents of children with SNE and disabilities who do not seem to benefit from FPE. Moreover, there is an established relationship between disability and poverty (WHO, 2011), so the parents of learners with SNE might require more assistance than the average parent. Creation of awareness on SNE and IE should be done so as to win public support. Due to limited resources, schools could be grouped together to share scarce personnel and other materials which may be in short supply. For instance, human resources like various therapists, audiologist and other paraprofessionals could serve more than one school. An IE policy should be created in order to guide practice and ensure uniformity across the country.

5   Conclusion and Recommendations

In this chapter, I have discussed the policy and legislative journey that Kenya has taken from pure segregation of learners with special needs and disabilities towards inclusive education. I have noted efforts from the Kenyan government to ensure success of IE, including guidelines for inclusive education. Challenges faced in defining IE have been highlighted since, what constitutes an inclusive education varies depending on the authority in question. As a result, I have argued that practice differs from one jurisdiction to another. In Kenya, there seems to be political will to ensure that IE succeeds in Kenya given the level of investment so far. Policies and legislation governing education have been discussed, giving prominence to their contributions to education for learners with SNE especially inclusion.

Pro-inclusive education practices proposed in policy and discussed include the Digital Literacy Programme (DLP), free primary education, creation of awareness in special and inclusive education, educational assessment for SNE and disabilities among others. Notably, the DLP will go a long way to include all learners especially those with learning difficulties and sensory impairments through application of technology in teaching and learning. Content can be presented to learners in modes that are compatible with their learning styles. Challenges identified include insufficient teaching and non-teaching personnel, limited skills, poor infrastructure and equipment for learners with SNE, and corruption which affect policy implementation.

This chapter proposes more support for learners with special needs and disabilities and their parents; sharing of resources among institutions to cover for limited human and material resources; government assistance to children with SNE and disabilities; minimizing corruption to ensure that funds reach are used for the intended purposes; and availing sufficient therapy services to learners. Implementing propositions in current policies would move the country much closer to inclusive practice in education.

References

Ainscow, M. (2005). Understanding the development of inclusive education system. *Electronic Journal of Research in Psychology, 3*(3), 5–20.

Ambaa, C. (2013). *Analysis of the Kenyan 8-4-4 system of education in relation to aims of education for self-reliance* (Unpublished master thesis). University of Nairobi, Kenya.

Armstrong, A. C., Armstrong, D., & Spandagou, I. (2010). *Inclusive education international policy and practice*. London: Sage Publications.

Cawthon, W. S. (2001). Teaching strategies in inclusive classes with deaf students. *Journal of Deaf Studies and Deaf Education, 6*(3), 212–225.

Chang'ach, J. K. (2013). Educational reforms in Kenya for innovation. *International Journal of Humanities and Social Science, 3*(9), 123–145.

Crossley, M. (2012). Comparative education and research capacity building: Reflections on international transfer and the significance of context. *Journal of International and Comparative Education, 1*(1), 4–12.

Frederickson, N., & Cline, T. (2002). *Special educational needs, inclusion and diversity: A text book*. Buckingham: Open University Press.

Government of Kenya (GoK). (2007). *Vision 2030*. Nairobi: Government Printers.

House of Commons. (2006). *Special educational needs: Third report of session 1 2005–2006*. London: The Stationery Office Ltd. Retrieved from http://www.publications.parliament.uk/pa/cm200506/cmselect/cmeduski/478/478i.pdf

Jarvis, J., Iantaffi, A., & Sinka, I. (2003). Inclusion in mainstream classrooms: Experiences of deaf pupils. In M. Nind, J. Sheehy, & K. Simmons (Eds.), *Inclusive education: Diverse perspectives*. London: David Fulton Publishers.

Jenkins, R., & Barr, E. (2006). *Social exclusion of scheduled caste children from primary education in India*. New Delhi: The United Nations Children's Fund (UNICEF). Retrieved from http://www.unicef.org/policyanalysis/files/Social_Exclusion_of_Scheduled_Caste_Children_from_Primary_Education_in_India.pdf

Kavua, M. K. (2014). *Communication strategies for deaf learners in inclusive settings*. Saarbrucken: Lambert Academic Publishing.

SPECIAL AND INCLUSIVE EDUCATION POLICY AND PRACTICE IN KENYA 115

Kenya Education Sector Support Programme (KESSP). (2005–2010). Retrieved from http://www.education.go.ke.MOESTDOCS/FINALPT1 July26205.pdf

Kenya National Human Rights Commission (KNHRC). (2014). *From norm to practice: A status report on implementation of the rights of persons with disabilities in Kenya.* Nairobi: KNHCR.

Martini, M. (2012). *Kenya: Overview of corruption and anti-corruption.* Retrieved from file:///C:/Users/user%20pc/Desktop/CORRUPTION_KENYA.pdf

Ministry of Education Science and Technology (MOEST). (2003). *A report of the taskforce on special needs education: Appraisal exercise, Kochung report.* Nairobi: Government Printers.

Ministry of Education Science and Technology (MOEST). (2005). *Delivering quality equitable education and training to all Kenyans.* Nairobi: MOEST.

Ministry of Education Science and Techsnology (MOEST). (2007). *Gender policy in education.* Nairobi: MOEST.

Ministry of Education Science and Technology (MOEST). (2009). *The national special needs education policy framework.* Nairobi: MOEST.

Ministry of Education Science and Technology (MOEST). (2013). *The basic education act no. 14 of 2013.* Retrieved from http://www.education.go.ke

Ministry of Information, Communication and Technology. (2015). *Digital literacy programme: Press statement on the digital literacy programme by Dr. Fred Matiang'i, cabinet secretary, ministry of information, science and technology delivered on 22nd June 2015, at the ministry of ICT boardroom.* Retrieved from http://www.icta.go.ke/downloads/digital_literacy_program_launch.pdf

National Association of Schoolmasters Union of Women Teachers (NASUWT). (2008). *Special education needs and inclusion: Reflection and renewal.* Birmingham: NASUWT.

National Council for Law Reporting. (2001). *The children act* (Revised ed. 2007). Nairobi: National Council for Law Reporting.

Nation Media Group. (2016, September 30). *The digital literacy programme.* Nairobi: Nation Media Group.

Ngaroga, J. M. (1996). *PTE revision series: Education for Primary Teacher Education.* Nairobi: East African Educational Publishers.

Ntarangwi, M. (2003). The challenges of education and development in post-colonial Kenya. *Africa Development, 28*(3–4), 211–228.

Nthia, O. N. (2009). *Constraints facing inclusive education for children with special needs in public primary schools in Embu East district, Embu County, Kenya* (Unpublished master dissertation). School of Education, Kenyatta University, Nairobi.

Powers, S. (2002). From concepts to practice in deaf education: A United Kingdom perspective on inclusion. *Journal of Deaf Studies and Deaf Education, 7*(3), 230–243.

Randiki, F. (2002). *Historical development of special needs.* Nairobi: KISE/UNISE Press.

Ravindran, N., & Myers, B. J. (2012). Cultural influences on the influence of health, illness and disability: A review and focus on autism. *Springer Science and Business Media, 21*(2), 311–319.

Republic of Kenya. (1964a). *Kenya education commission report, Ominde report.* Nairobi: Government Press.

Republic of Kenya. (1964b). *The committee on care and rehabilitation of the disabled, Ngala Mwendwa report.* Nairobi: Government Printers.

Republic of Kenya. (1965). *Sessional paper no. 10 of 1965.* Nairobi: Government Printers.

Republic of Kenya. (1976). *Report of the national committee on educational objectives and policies, Gachathi report.* Nairobi: Government Press.

Republic of Kenya. (1981). *The presidential working party on the second university, Mackay report.* Nairobi: Government Printers.

Republic of Kenya. (1988). *The presidential working party on education and manpower: Kamunge report.* Nairobi: Government Printers.

Republic of Kenya. (1999). *The commission of inquiry into the education system of Kenya: Koech commission.* Nairobi: Government Printers.

Republic of Kenya. (2001). *The children's act: Number 8 of 2001.* Nairobi: National Council for Law Reporting.

Republic of Kenya. (2003a). *A report of the taskforce on special needs education: Appraisal exercise.* Nairobi: Ministry of Education, Science and Technology.

Republic of Kenya. (2003b). *Persons with disabilities act.* Nairobi: National Council for Law Reporting.

Republic of Kenya. (2005b). *Ministry of gender, sports, culture and social services: Sessional paper no. 5 of 2005 on gender equality and development.* Nairobi: Government Printers.

Republic of Kenya. (2010). *Constitution of Kenya.* Nairobi: National Council for Law Reporting.

Republic of Kenya. (2013). *Basic education act.* Nairobi: Government printers.

Riddell, S., & Watson, N. (Eds.). (2003). *Disability, culture and identity.* Essex: Pearson.

Sifuna, D. N., & Otiende, E. J. (1994). *An introduction history of education* (Revised ed.). Nairobi: Nairobi University Press.

Simiyu, J. W. (2001). *Factors, which influence the teaching of technical and vocational subjects in primary schools in Uasin Gishu district* (Unpublished master dissertation). Moi University, Eldoret.

Transparency International. (2010). *Kenya education sector integrity study results.* Nairobi: Transparency International Kenya.

UNESCO. (1994). *Salamanca statement and framework for action on special needs education.* Paris: The United Nations Educational, Scientific and Cultural Organization (UNESCO).

UNESCO. (2000). *Dakar framework for action. Education for all: Meeting our collective agreements.* Paris: The United Nations Educational, Scientific and Cultural Organization (UNESCO).

UNESCO. (2005). *Guidelines for inclusion: Ensuring access to education for all.* Paris: The United Nations Educational, Scientific and Cultural Organization (UNESCO).

UNESCO. (2007, July 23–27). *Poverty alleviation, HIV and AIDS education and inclusive education: Priority issues for inclusive quality education in Eastern and Western Sub Saharan Africa.* Paper presented at the Regional Seminar, Nairobi, Kenya.

UNESCO. (2009). *Policy guidelines on inclusion in education.* Paris: The United Nations Educational, Scientific and Cultural Organization (UNESCO).

United Nations. (2006). *The United Nations Convention for the Rights of Persons with Disabilities and optional protocol (UNCRPD).* Retrieved from http://www.un.org/disabilities/documents/convention/convoptprot-e.pdf

World Health Organization (WHO). (2011). *World report on disability.* Valletta: WHO.

CHAPTER 7

In-Service Tutor Development in Support of Inclusive Education: Lessons from Partnerships between University and Organizations

Lawrence Eron

1 Historical Context

The last two decades has been significant in development of special needs and inclusive education in Uganda. Teacher training was initiated in 1988 particularly focusing on preparing teachers for the primary level of education. It followed a long period of having children with different disabilities and other special needs being taught by teachers trained outside Uganda or within the country through short courses by voluntary organisations. The Primary Teacher Education was targeted and in-service tutor training identified as the gateway. The centralized training of teachers was implemented at the then Uganda National Institute of Special Education (UNISE) now Kyambogo University. It was done alongside the decentralized early identification, assessment, placement and referral through the Special Needs Education/Educational Assessment and Resource Services (SNR/ERAS) programme.

As the training expanded, Uganda was also coping with new developments and trends within the special needs education especially towards inclusive education. Inclusive education is a feasible strategy for ensuring Education for *all*. But it was clear that its implementation should be in tandem with the socio-cultural, political and economic contexts. It was apparent that the key to inclusive education would focus on reforms within teacher development. It was therefore necessary to recognize partnerships as a means of expanding inclusive training.

2 Inclusive Education in Uganda

Inclusive education has been adopted worldwide as the best strategy to ensure that all children access quality and equitable education. In Uganda, the commitment is demonstrated by the legal (GoU, 2006) and non-legal frameworks on education and the establishment of educational infrastructure aimed at mainstreaming disability (Emong & Eron, 2016). Similarly, increasing numbers

© KONINKLIJKE BRILL NV, LEIDEN, 2019 | DOI:10.1163/9789004391505_008

of children with disabilities (CWD) are enrolled in mainstream schools, however their attendance, completion and transition rates and levels of achievement tend to be very low (Moyi, 2012). Teacher education and other training programmes related to supporting special needs and inclusive education are offered at Kyambogo University. However, there are systematic challenges that relate to recruitment, deployment, remuneration and support to ensure effectiveness. Emerging studies have indicated that this problematic situation is compounded by many factors including and not limited to lack of commitment of teachers, inadequate education infrastructure, prevalent negative social attitudes, overcrowded classrooms, and shortage of necessary teaching and learning resources in schools (Arbeiter & Hartley, 2002; Najingo, 2004; Nyende, 2012). All these factors impact on the role of the teacher in support for inclusive education.

Inclusive education requires teacher educators to accept the responsibility for preparing students who can support all children to learn and feel a sense of belonging. According to Blanton et al. (2011), one of the greatest critiques of teacher education is the need for increased and aligned clinical experiences that should be situated in inclusive settings. In this task, in-service tutor development is being adopted because of the central role it plays in shaping the minds of pre-service and in-service teachers.

This chapter is located within the recent developments in inclusive education and the broader discussion about the role of teachers in educating all children more effectively than may have been done in the past. The tutor development strategy considers broad issues of underachievement and participation, and the roles, responsibilities, as well as skills and knowledge of tutors. It focuses on teacher capacity and commitment, to offering quality training to student teachers who in turn will facilitate inclusive education (IE) for children with disabilities and other special needs.

3 Conceptual Framework

A wealth of literature provides a conceptual framework for understanding the development and nature of university-development partnership strategy towards inclusive education. These focused on the importance of promoting inclusive education through teacher development and partnership in professional teacher development.

3.1 *Promoting Inclusive Education through Teacher Development*
There are recent developments and discussions on inclusive education particularly about the role of teachers in educating *all* children more

effectively than may have been done in the past. The strategy is to ensure that tutor development broadly accommodates the roles, responsibilities, skills and knowledge for underachievement and participation of learners. It focuses on teacher capacity and commitment, to offering quality training to student teachers who in turn will facilitate inclusive education (IE) for children with disabilities and other special needs. UNESCO (2013) documents studies conducted in Uganda about teacher development, recruitment, deployment, absenteeism, teacher attrition, remuneration, and opportunities for career development, job satisfaction and recommends existing context for social dialogue. According to Ward, Penny, and Read (2006) political will, decentralization, funding and change of mind-set are contributing factors. However, the impressive quantitative gains often report face challenges of not keeping pace with ensuring quality learning outcomes, dropout and repetitions. Kasirye (2009) contends that limited information is available on how successful pupils are educated due to paucity of the data. Even the available data is often generalized with little specific reference on the categories of the special needs in children (Eron, 2015).

The distinction between professional development and teacher development is not highlighted in the literature but is worth considering (Mann, 2005). According to Mann, professional teacher development should be more inclusive taking into consideration personal, moral and teaching dimensions. Tomlinson (2003) contends that teacher development approach within a teacher education programme helps to develop a 'multi-dimensional awareness' and 'the ability to apply this awareness to the actual contexts of teaching'. This argument is necessary to explain the intention of the programme and the purpose of the partnership arrangement. Partnerships contribute to identifying and providing resources that facilitate in-service developments of teachers. It demonstrates the important that pre-service teachers are encouraged to develop professionally (Damron, 2005).

Damron's (2005) assertion is the basis for most of the developed countries to spend a great deal of their gross national income in various ways on the education and training of human resources in order to survive, develop and progress (Ahmadi & Keshavarzi, 2013). This survival, development and progress is demonstrated through the methods, skills and attitudes that teaches demonstrate in their self-development. According to Mann (2005) self-development is a measure that taken takes into consideration to of a large extent of self-direction. The aim the process is to match the current pupil enrolment projection to teacher presence and performance. This is done in recognition that nearly half of the Ugandan population is below the age of 5 years and the population structure is expected to remain youthful for the next fifteen years.

TABLE 7.1   Evolution of the school aged population, 2010–2025

Total	2010	2015	2020	2025	2025/2010
Population	31,784,320	37,906,700	45,056,717	53,645,446	Ratio 1.7
3–5 years	3,651,770	4,441,890	5,092,124	6,013,077	1.6
6–12 years	6,538,950	8,317,330	10,588,112	13,473,293	2.1
13–16 years	2,966,970	3,539,910	4,396,614	5,352,059	1.8
17–18 years	1,368,310	1,526,320	1,611,902	1,749,507	1.3
Total 6–18 years	10,874,230	13,383,560	16,596,627	20,574,859	1.9
Total 6–18 years (%)	34.2%	35.3%	36.8%	38.4%	

SOURCE: MOES (TIISA-2013)

While these projections are indicative figures for planning, the figures are generalizable. The assumption is that the population of children with disabilities and other special needs follow suit. The lack of segregation calls for a strategic planning for them as in most cases right to education for students with disabilities in Uganda is still suffering from discrimination (Emong & Eron, 2016).

3.2   *Partnership in Professional Teacher Development*

The need for a more inclusive learning outcomes experiences has led the university to partner with development organizations to rethink way they can work together in teacher and programme development. The tutor development programme was developed as a partnership project between Kyambogo University and Sight Savers Uganda country office. Other partners included the Ministry of Education and Sports, Uganda Society for Disabled Children and the National Union of Disabled Children. The intent of involving all these partners is to increased ownership and promote its sustainability. The project is to ensure that inclusive education to the benefit of every child in the school through to among other things:

1. Increasing the capacity and commitment of primary teacher educators (tutors) to offer training in inclusive education (IE) for children with disabilities
2. Increasing the capacity and commitment of newly-trained primary teachers nationwide to include children with disabilities in their classes
3. Ensuring that children with disabilities and their families across Uganda benefit from improved and an inclusive education in mainstream schools

The target beneficiaries are projected to cascade from teacher educators to learners as outlined in Table 7.2.

TABLE 7.2   Beneficiaries

Group of beneficiaries	Male	Female	Total
Specialist tutors in primary teachers colleges	50	58	108
Selected coordinating center tutors	20	26	46
Trainee teachers in primary teachers colleges	15,200	19,000	34,200[a]
Other tutors in primary teachers colleges	900	1,180	2,080
Other coordinating center tutors (CCTs)	210	244	454
Principals and deputy principals of the primary teachers colleges	60	48	108
Inspectors of schools	300	200	500
Practicing teachers under CCT catchment areas	29,000	31,000	60,000

a At the end of the project expected number of trainees graduating with knowledge in special needs and inclusive education.

Indirectly the in-service tutor development will benefit:
- All children and their families across Uganda from improved quality and inclusive education in mainstream schools
- Classroom teachers and other education personnel across Uganda interested in facilitating an inclusive class who will be able to download the information education and communication (IEC) materials from the project website to help them improve on their practice
- Community based organisations and other scholars elsewhere interested in learning best practices from the IEC materials shared on the project website to enable them adapt to their own practices.

Three key questions are focused in this chapter:
- What capacity is in place for training pre-service and in-service teachers in special needs and inclusive education?
- What support is given to promote learning, participation and development as a means of reducing drop out of students with disabilities and other special needs?
- What modifications could be in place to promote inclusive education training and practices?

3.3   In-Service Tutor Development Process

The implementation of the programme took different processes. After the conceptualization of the programme, a baseline survey was undertaken to establish the situation on the ground. This was followed by the development of the training curriculum that guided the production of the training materials.

Thereafter the training was centrally done with a clear guideline of who should be admitted for the training. Cascading plan and implementation strategies were developed as a means of ensuring that the targeted child with disabilities and other special needs benefits.

4 Baseline Survey

For effective implementation of the project, a baseline survey was undertaken to identify best practices that needed to build on and the challenges that should guide the training and other implementation plans. Eight Primary Teachers' Colleges (four Core Colleges and four Pre-service Colleges)[1] were selected. These were Colleges selected because they had students with disabilities admitted or where the special needs distance education programme being offered. A tutor from each college who is teaching the special needs, seven students without disabilities and a student with disability were consulted. Details about participant characteristics are presented in Table 7.3.

TABLE 7.3   Participant characteristics

Participants	No. per college	No. total	Method
Tutors	1	8	Individual interview
Students with disabilities	1	8	Individual interview
Students without disabilities	7	56	Focus group discussion

The information gathered from them highlighted factors relating to enrolment, drop-out and progression of students in the colleges, how functional assessment was being carried out, adaptation being made and use of curriculum materials, development of alternative communication skills, modification made in the school environment as well as professional and training gaps. Information generated from this baseline survey shaped the development of training materials and eventual tutor training.

5 Development of Training Materials

The training of teachers started with the development and accreditation of the curriculum done by Kyambogo University as a fully-fledged Certificate in Special Needs and Inclusive Education. The training curriculum provided for eleven (11) theoreti-

TABLE 7.4   Topics covered

i. Introduction to disability and other special needs,	vi. Assessment of learning needs
ii. Policy and development of special needs and inclusive education,	vii. Learning and teaching braille
	viii. Learning and teaching Ugandan sign language
iii. Child rights protection for children with disabilities	ix. Working with stakeholders towards inclusive education
iv. Early identification and intervention	x. Teaching in an inclusive class
v. Communication for learners with special needs	xi. Practicum

cal and practical courses. Ten (10) of the courses had modules focusing on content found in the Primary Teacher Education syllabus and additional content aimed at broadening tutor understanding and awareness of contemporary inclusive practices. The eleventh course was purely practical where tutor students worked with student teachers and the community to popularize inclusive learning. A facilitator's guide was also developed to inform the tutors on step by step process of using the modules. The modules had content covers topics as seen in Table 7.4.

General and specific equipment for the training were identified by Kyambogo University, procured by Sight Savers and distributed to all participating colleges. In addition, supplementary materials for teaching braille and sign language were produced. Sign language videos for example, focused on content relevant for primary school content.

6 The Training Processes

The training programme had three stages:

Stage One

The first step involved the orientation of the facilitators on adult learning and how to adapt to distance mode of delivery. The orientation provided synergy on how the facilitators would operate and helped harmonise the time table. It was also a refresher training to understand the Primary Teacher Education Curriculum so that they refer to it during the training.

Stage Two

This involved the training of two tutors identified from all Primary Teachers' Colleges (PTCS) in Uganda at the time.[2] Two tutors were admitted from each of the government aided and privately-owned PTCs[3] making a total of 108 candidates. The criteria for admission was that the tutors should be teaching Professional Education Studies.[4]

Tutors with special needs education background were given priority to reorient them to inclusive education. To support the training, the College Principals and Deputy Principals were trained/oriented. The orientation of these mangers which was done at different intervals was to introduce them to inclusive education, ensure proper and careful selection of the tutors to be trained, coordinate and monitor performance at college level.

The training of tutors was centrally done in one college. The training had three parts. The first were three face-to-face sessions of one week each. During each of the weeks, tutors were oriented to the modules and given action-oriented assignments to carry out while taking individual study.

FIGURE 7.1 Training session for braille writing and reading

FIGURE 7.2 Training session for sign language

The second part was individual study of the modules and carrying out the activities provided to them during the face to face. Each module had its own activity that was compiled by the tutor students, marked and feedback given by the facilitators. The third phase involved a practicum following the action plan that each college group developed. The action plans were discussed with the facilitators and approved from which a report would be written.

Stage Three

The third stage was the practicum that involved training of students on inclusive education. The tutor trainees also cascaded the training to fellow tutors in their colleges. The intent of cascading the training among tutors was to enable each staff teach their subject with an inclusive orientation. It was also to make sure that the needs of students with disabilities are identified and attended to both in and out of class. Involvement of all staff implied student teachers would be supported to plan, teach, assess and support their learning during practice and hopefully after completion with an inclusive dimension.

7 Emerging Issues

In carrying through the planning, identification of tutors and training to meet the targeted objectives, there were a number of positive factors that can be registered as opportunities for the programme:

i. There was excitement among the participants as their training provided solutions to the challenges they faced in their classes and when they follow student teachers for support supervision.

ii. The distance learning mode of delivery motivated the tutors to take responsibility for their own learning and practice. They had opportunity to be supported by Kyambogo University staff, acquire reference materials and training equipment that were needed for their practice with students.

iii. Involvement of two tutors from the same college was considered an opportunity as they would share experiences. The tutors reported that where they did not have adequate knowledge and skills, the colleagues were there to consult.

iv. The tutors reported that it was possible to ensure reasonable accommodation in an inclusive setting with minimal resources. Their change of attitude during and after the training caused a lot of transformation in the way they teach and work with students and others.

Some of challenging issues that the programme had to cope with included:

i. Some colleges did not follow the criterial for nominating tutors for sponsorship. The identified tutors were not teaching the professional education studies. This implied that they will have to be allocated additional load to implement the special need and inclusive education skills.

ii. Some tutors withdrew from the programme for various reasons. While others went for postgraduate studies, others lost interest after realizing that they would not be paid allowances for training. The distance mode of delivery was similar to workshops that they often attended and paid for. Therefore, of the 108 admitted only 101 completed the programme.

iii. There were many concurrent programmes that necessitated the attention of the same tutors. While others were examiners (involved in central marking of student end of year examinations), other tutors were facilitators on other educational reforms. Their interests helped them complete the progamme.

8 Lessons Learnt

The conceptualization of the in-service tutor development programme was based on the changing trends and strategies towards inclusion and inclusive education. These strategies are consistent to the need for strong collaborations between government, its agencies and development partners. The recognition is that the provision of inclusive education is possible when teachers are well equipped with knowledge, skills and attitudes. The partnership between Kyambogo University and Sight Savers Country Office is strategic testimony that teacher education is a collaborative process.

There is evidence that special needs and inclusive education is gaining ground in Uganda. Iinstitutions and development partners have the will, however, for it to be deep rooted, there are political, economic, social and technological conditions that needs to be addressed. For instance, there is need for a policy to guide inclusive education principles and practices. Therefore, a well-structured teacher development programme will fill the gap quality teachers (Nyende, 2012) towards inclusion and financing of special needs and inclusive education programmes (CSBAG, 2013) which are very important for successful adjustment and inclusion of students with disabilities and other special needs.

During the process of the in-service tutor training, a number of challenges and strategies for improvement identified included:

i   the need for modification in functional assessment, adaptation of curriculum materials, development of alternative communication skills and modification of college environment.

ii   Openly and constantly talking about issues relating to education of students with disabilities and other special educational needs at college and school levels. These discussions will allow for planning and giving time to individual special needs.

iii   Special Needs Education was a course hidden under Professional Educational Studies affecting its visibility. The special needs and Inclusive education course should be an independent subject taught to all students and skills developed assessed in all students. Considering that everybody has varying level of special needs, teaching it as a core subject benefits not only students but the whole education system.

iv   Inclusive education is practical when adequate attention is paid to the needs of students with disabilities and other special educational needs enrolled in the colleges. The starting point is the recruitment of tutors trained in special needs and inclusive education. This would be followed by each college coming up with institutional policy to provide for reasonable accommodation as a means of ensuring inclusive education

v   There is still need for more sensitisation among education planners, implementers and partners to ensure that awareness about the needs of students with disabilities are emphasized. Mentorship to college staff and students on issues relating to disability inclusion and inclusive education would be the best sensitisation strategy. In doing so, a more organised assessment processes and records are developed to inform planning for inclusion in all colleges.

9   Conclusion

It is the considered belief of the author that in-service teacher development is an effective means of solving segregated service provision. Ultimately, this training and its cascading to the student teachers is basic and will still require support from specialized trained teachers in the school whose roles would be defined. Through an inclusive teacher education all educational reforms will take into consideration special educational needs of learners who are often marginalized because of their disabilities or other factors. The author hopes that the experiences from this approach, including the materials used for tutor development, would be absorbed into the teacher education system in Uganda and many other countries who are struggling with inclusive education. Teacher education is the only entry point to realizing the goal for education for all.

Notes

1   A Core College offers both in-service and Pre-service training while a Pre-service focus on direct entrants to the teaching profession).
2   The number of private Primary Teachers' Colleges has since increased from the original 54 (2016) making a total of 62 PTCs (2018) In Uganda.
3   Liberalisation of education provide for privately owned teachers' colleges operating alongside government but should affiliate to and be centrally accredited by Kyambogo University.
4   Professional Education Studies covers teaching methods, curriculum and special needs education.

References

Ahmadi, S., & Keshavarzi, A. (2013). A survey of in-service training programs effectiveness in teaching skills development from the view-point of students, teachers and principals of guidance schools in Shiraz. *Procedia – Social and Behavioral Sciences, 83*, 920–925.
Arbeiter, S., & Hartley, S. (2002). Teachers' and pupils' experiences of integrated education in Uganda. *International Journal of Disability, Development and Education, 49*(1), 61–78.

Blanton, L. P., Pugach, M. C., & Florian, L. (2011). *Preparing general education teachers to improve outcomes for students with disabilities*. Retrieved from http://www.aacte.org

CSBAG. (2013). *Financing special needs education in Uganda: Tracking flow of funds for special needs in Abim, Kibale and Agago districts*. Kampala: Civil Society Budget Advocacy Group/Democratic Governance Facility.

Damron, J. (2005). Encouraging professional development on pre-service teachers. *The Teacher Trainer, 19*(1), 3–6.

Emong, P., & Eron, L. (2016). Disability inclusion in higher education in Uganda: Status and strategies. *African Journal of Disability, 5*(1), a193. Retrieved from http://dx.doi. org/10.4102/ajod.v5i1.193

Eron, L. (2015). *Educating teachers of the deaf: Experiences and perspectives from teachers on facilitating academic and social participation in Uganda*. Oslo: Akademika Publishing.

GoU. (2006). *The persons with disabilities act*. Kampala: UPPC. Retrieved from https://news.mak.ac.ug/documents.makfiles/theses/najjigo_Hellen.pdf

Kasirye, I. (2009). *Determinants of learning achievements in Uganda*. Retrieved from http://www.csae.ox.ac.uk/conferences/2009-EdiA/papers/325-Kasirye.pdf

Mann, S. (2005). The language teacher's development. *Language Teaching, 38*, 103–118. doi:10.1017/S0261444805002867

Moyi, P. (2012). Access to education for children with disabilities in Uganda: Implications for education for all. *Journal of International Education and Leadership, 2*(2), 1–13. Retrieved from http://www.jielusa.og/home/

Najingo, H. (2004). *Challenges of accessing all-inclusive education services by children with disabilities: A case study of Mijwala sub-county Sembabule district* (Unpublished masters thesis). Makerere University, Kampala.

Nyende, F. (2012). *Children with disabilities in universal primary education in Uganda: A rights-based analysis to inclusive education*. Retrieved from http://hdl.handle.net/2105/13189

Tomlinson, C. (2003). *Fulfilling the promise of the differentiated classroom: Strategies and tools for responsive teaching*. Alexandria, VA: Association for Supervision and Curriculum Development.

UNESCO. (2013). *Teacher issues in Uganda: A shared vision for an effective teachers policy*. Kampala: Ministry of Education and Sports. Retrieved from http://www.teachersforefa.unesco.org/v2/phocadownload/Country_Support/tissa_uganda_full_report.pdf

Ward, M., Penny, A., & Read, T. (2006). *Education reform in Uganda – 1997 to 2004: Reflections on policy, partnerships, strategy and implementation* (Vol. 60). London: DFID.

CHAPTER 8

Inclusive Education Policy Implementation in Swaziland: A Critical Reflection on Developments Since 2011

Cebsile P. Nxumalo

1 Introduction

During the past 37 years, there has been international interest in the inclusion of children with special needs in regular schools (Ballard, 1998; Booth & Ainscow, 1998; Ainscow, 1999). Prior to this, children with special needs were educated in special schools and institutions and separated from their peers. The perception that education should be provided to all children regardless of their differences and needs led to the development of inclusive education. The concept of inclusive education was strengthened in the 1990s (e.g. UNESCO, 1994), and it brought a renewed promise for all children with special needs to be treated as individuals who have equal rights to education. Inclusive education is based on the notion of equality and equity. It promotes education for all children regardless of differences, challenges and abilities and it maintains a vision of a school for all. Furthermore, inclusive education accepts all children as they are, providing them with relevant and adequate resources and support according to their specific needs (UNESCO, 1994). It is also concerned with the conditions under which children can be educated effectively (Barton, 1997) and that schools should review the organization and provision of the curriculum in order to effectively respond to all learners as individuals. Since the proclamation of the Salamanca Statement (1994) and the Dakar Framework for Action (2000) several countries have been improving their education systems and making remarkable efforts towards inclusive education. In light of this, Swaziland, has been working on the notion of including every learner with special needs and disabilities in general education classrooms for nearly eighteen years. In April, 2011 the Ministry of Education and Training adopted the Swaziland Education and Training Sector Policy (EDSEC). An important component of this policy was that it adopted inclusive education as a policy approach at all the levels of the education system from pre-primary to tertiary education.

This chapter, therefore, reflects on developments that have shaped the understandings, definitions and implementation of inclusive education

---

© KONINKLIJKE BRILL NV, LEIDEN, 2019 | DOI:10.1163/9789004391505_009

in Swaziland since the 2011 EDSEC policy came into force. It highlights current meanings and local understandings of inclusion and how these have influenced policy frameworks and practice. The notion of inclusive education as an approach to provide quality education for all children regardless of differences is explored (Engelbrecht, 2006; Miles & Singal, 2010). The chapter further reflects on how Swaziland is engaging with inclusive education, given the contextual socio-economic constraints and possibilities and the tensions, contradictions and complexities that have fraught implementation of inclusive education in many countries (Slee, 2006; Spurgeon, 2007; Miles & Singal, 2010). The chapter concludes with key recommendations for further development of inclusive education in this context.

2　Historical Background to Inclusive Education at International, Continental and Regional Levels

Understanding the origins of special education and its historical background at international, continental and regional levels forms a basis for understanding possible influences within the Swaziland context. Tracing the history of inclusive education at international level reveals that this view has evolved from a series of stages in development originating from special education to inclusive education, which has been justified from both a human rights approach and from the view point of effectiveness (Ainscow, 2007; UNESCO, 2003b).

Prior to 1980, terms such as 'education for all' and 'inclusion' were not part of the special education language and engagement (Armstrong, Armstrong, & Spandagou, 2010). Historically speaking, children with special needs were excluded from the educational system before the 1970s (Balescut & Eklindh, 2006). Categories such as 'handicap' or 'disability' were reinforced over the years through various forms of legislation which recognized the differences between individuals and the need for separate education where children should be taught according to 'age ability and aptitude'. According to Armstrong, Armstrong, and Spandagou (2010), special education served the interests of the mainstream sector by removing troublesome children and those who were not progressing well in school. By the 1970s there was a gradual shift which consisted of specialized programs, institutions and specialist educators which however, functioned parallel to the mainstream education system (Ainscow, 2007).

Eventually in the late 1970s there was discontent with special education which developed a new approach, namely special needs education which consisted of different approaches including integration of children with disabilities within ordinary schools and in specialized classrooms or sharing several hours of the same class with their non-disabled peers. Emphasis shifted significantly with the Warnock Committee's recommendations for special education provision particularly within special schools, remedial units and other institutions, to support the needs of individual learners within different categories of 'special needs'. The abolishment of categories of handicap in favor of the new term 'special educational needs', was recommended and emphasis was placed on assessing an individual's special educational need or learning difficulty. The Warnock Report of 1978 had great influence in subsequent development of special educational policy and practice (Armstrong, Armstrong, & Spandagou, 2010). The report critiqued the high number of children failing within the mainstream schools and also critiqued the whole school system. The Warnock Report was seen within an overall context of an attempt to construct a more rational framework for identifying and dealing with children failing in or failed by the mainstream school system (Armstrong, Armstrong, & Spandagou, 2010).

The move towards greater support for children with a range of special needs, including those with disabilities, was as a result of a resounding emphasis on the need to recognize and respond to human rights (UN Human Rights Convention, 1949). This was followed by a focus specifically on the rights of the child (UN Convention on the Rights of the Child), and then the right to education for all (Education for all, Jomtien, 1990). In terms of special needs there was a move towards ensuring that all children had a right to education in their local neighborhood schools (Salamanca Conference, 1994). The Salamanca Statement became the drive to the concept of inclusive education suggesting radical changes to the form of integration, which was to accept a diverse range of special needs or excluded groups but not only limited to disabilities (UNESCO, 1994). Since the Salamanca Statement, current thinking about inclusion in many countries has moved the emphasis from simply integration or mainstreaming which is about simply placing children with disabilities and special needs into mainstream schools and supporting them so they can fit into current policies and practices as they exist. This shift in thinking supported an emphasis on human rights and children's rights led to non-discriminatory practices. The right to inclusive education for persons with disabilities was also given full recognition through Article 24 of the UN Convention on the Rights of Persons with Disabilities (2006) which demands for the provision of education for persons with disabilities in an education system that is inclusive and responsive to the needs of all.

The commitment to realize the right to education of children with disabilities as prescribed by international frameworks was embraced by continental leaders including Swaziland leaders. The leaders' commitment was evident in the adoption of the African Decade of the Disabled Persons (ADDP) (1999–2009) with the African Union (AU) Continental Plan of Action for Persons with Disabilities which focuses on critical areas of importance on equalizing opportunities for people with disabilities in all areas of society, including education. The extended African Union (AU) Continental Plan of Action for Persons with Disabilities (2019) has made provision for special measures to be put in place towards addressing the needs of children with disabilities, including ensuring that they have access to all levels of the education system. In addition, the Plan commits member states to: "Establish policies to ensure that girls and boys with disabilities have access to relevant education in integrated settings at all levels, paying particular attention to the requirements of children in rural areas" (African Union [AU] Continental Plan of Action on the African Decade of Persons with Disabilities, 2012). Furthermore, the African Charter on the Rights and Welfare of the Child (1999) commits members of the African Union to realise the right of every child to education. The Charter states that Member States should take special measures in respect of female, gifted and disadvantaged children, to ensure equal access to education for all sections of the community.

In addition, the Southern Africa Development Community (SADC) adopted a Framework and Programme of Action (2008–2015) for Comprehensive Care and Support for Orphans, Vulnerable Children, and Youth in SADC. This framework has a vision aimed at ensuring that the rights and basic needs of all children and youth in the SADC region are fully met and able to grow up well to realize their full human potential. Its main purpose is to integrate vulnerable children and youth in the SADC development agenda and has made it a priority at policy, legislative and intervention levels. It focuses on providing them with comprehensive services in a holistic manner. Children with special needs and disabilities are recognized as vulnerable children and targeted for specific attention through the activities driven by this Framework. In light of all the legal instruments, the inclusive education movement has become the cornerstone of education reform in countries of the world (Armstrong, Armstrong, & Spandagou, 2010; Holt, 2003), including Swaziland.

3   Inclusive Education Development in Swaziland

There have been key historical developments in policy in the Kingdom of Swaziland towards a framework for inclusion in practice. These policy developments have been influenced by all the international, continental and regional frameworks highlighted above. In addition to the aforementioned frameworks at a national level other frameworks include the Imbokodvo Manifesto of 1972; the 1999 National Policy Statement on Education and subsequent Education and Training Policy of 2011. In its 1972, after Independence Manifesto, the newly independent Monarchy of Swaziland prioritized education. The Philosophy, Policies and Objectives of the Imbokodvo National Movement known as the 'Imbokodvo Manifesto' of 1972 called for the right to education for all Swazi citizens notably this was way before the EFA, Jomtien Conference of 1990. Therefore, it worth noting that as early as 1972, the aspirations of the Swazi Government were that all Swazi citizens should be educated (1972). Education was seen as an inalienable right of every child and every citizen to receive to the limit of his/her capabilities. Universal Free Primary Education for every Swazi child was the ultimate goal of the Imbokodvo Manifesto. It is also worth noting that most of the policies that are followed today, including the education sector policy, are enshrined in the manifesto. Furthermore, the policy on 'education for all Swazi citizens' as espoused in the Imbokodvo Manifesto came into force twenty two years before the 1990 global call on Education for All. On another note, education for persons with disabilities started in 1967, a few years before the Imbokodvo Manifesto's existence.

Similar to other countries in the world, Special Education in Swaziland started as a charitable initiative by missionaries in particular the Roman Catholic Church with the establishment of a resource centre for physically disabled learners at St Joseph's Mission in 1967. In the same year, steps to establish the first Resource Centre for blind students were taken. St Joseph's then started integrating children with mental challenges at the Zama Centre. In 1974, the Roman Catholic Church also established Ekululameni Rehabilitation Training Centre at St Josephs' Mission. In 1975, through an initiative from the Society for the Handicapped, another school for children who had learning disabilities was established by two American Peace Corps volunteers in Mbabane. The school still exists and is now known as Ekwetsembeni Special School and is funded by the Ministry of Education and Training. The first centre for the education of the Deaf in Swaziland was established in 1975 by Irish Sisters (Catholic) on premises made available by the Enjabulweni Children's Home, with equipment and furniture provided by the Rotary Club of Manzini. The School for the Deaf came as a beacon of light to challenge ethnocentric attitudes and also strongly contributed towards the understanding of Deaf Culture as a concept which depicts the holistic spiritual assets of the Deaf Community, which include Sign Language as a primary language, shared values, customs and technology which are transferred from one generation to another. Not until, 1999, special education was comprehended as the only approach to provide education for learners with special needs and disabilities.

The move towards support for children and youth with special needs and disabilities in inclusive settings was largely influenced by the international declarations and agreements discussed above. National policies such as the 1999 National Education Policy Statement put a resounding emphasis on the right to education for all children including those with special needs. Through the 1999statement, the government of Swaziland pledged to address the needs of children with special needs within normal schools rather than creating dedicated facilities for them. However, it was only in 2006 that the National Education Policy Statement was implemented through a strategy which targeted nine primary schools. Among the nine schools, two schools had a rural and urban focus in each of the four geographical and administrative regions in Swaziland. These schools were designated as models of inclusion. Moreover, awareness raising and capacity building workshops were conducted for primary school teachers on how to cater for diversity in their classrooms. The aforementioned National Policy Statement of 1999 was only revised ten years later and in 2011 it came to force as the Swaziland Education and Training Sector (EDSEC) policy. This 2011 policy gave impetus to inclusive education, and it became a policy approach that informed planning and implementation at all levels of the education system.

With the release of the Education and Training Sector Policy (EDSEC) of 2011, the issues of inclusive education formed a growing part of the education system in Swaziland. The EDSEC brought a greater shift in thinking and practice in inclusive education in Swaziland. A unique direction was taken by the Swaziland MoET by mainstreaming IE into the body of the EDSEC policy and ensuring that IE is comprehensively addressed, monitored and reported. This mainstreaming approach eliminated the need for separate, free-standing policies on areas that are seen to be cross-cutting such as HIV and AIDS, Schools as Centres of Care and Support (SCCS) and Inclusive Education. In principle, this meant that attention to inclusive education and response management would be a routine function of the MoET at every level (MoET, 2011). Realistic inclusion demands that countries take such a holistic approach which involves all sub-sectors within the education system. For the purpose of the EDSEC, as is the case in Swaziland. The mainstreaming elucidated in the EDSEC policy of 2011 refers to the integration of related issues within the education sector such as inclusive education, HIV and AIDS, Schools of Centres of Care and Support (Inqaba) in the main body of the policy. The aim of using this approach was to avoid the proliferation of multiple, sub-sector policies which could lead to duplication and confusion. Furthermore, the EDSEC policy engrained the concept of Inqaba (CSTL), which means fortress – a safe haven for all learners, as an inclusive strategy to promote child-friendly education systems and schools

(MoET, 2011, p. 14). Notably, this is a clear indication that Swaziland changed the focus from the narrow view that inclusive education is only focusing on children with disabilities to a wider perspective as an approach towards overall quality education and removal of barriers to educational attainment for all (UNESCO, 2003).

4   Meanings and Definitions of Inclusive Education

To appreciate the influences on the development of inclusive education nationally, a discussion of the meaning and significance on inclusive education should be made concrete (Armstrong, Armstrong, & Spandagou, 2010). Moreso because Inclusive education has gained currency in theoretical debates and policy programming, however, it means different things to different people (Armstrong, Armstrong, & Spandagou, 2010, p. 28). Therefore by definition Inclusive Education (IE) remains ambiguous in different countries and amongst researchers (UNESCO, 2003a, 2005; Booth, 2005; Ainscow, 2000, 2007). However, most importantly, the principles of the Salamanca Statement, inclusion education has two fundamental objectives and roles. First and foremost, it means to accept excluded or disadvantaged children and youth with various special needs not just disabilities. Second, inclusion improves and enriches the quality of education in classrooms in a way that children with or without special needs learn from each other in a positive way and discriminatory attitudes are eliminated (UNESCO, 1994). The basic principle of inclusive education is a commitment to belonging, nurturing and educating all students regardless of their difference in ability, culture, gender, language, class and ethnicity (Kozelski, Artiles, Fletcher, & Engelbrecht, 2009).

While the inclusive education debate has undoubtedly played a significant role in raising concerns about disabled children in international and regional forums, it is important to understand it not as a philosophy or educational approach exclusively for children with disabilities, but as an approach that is fundamental to achieving the right to education for children from all marginalized groups (UNICEF, 2011, p. 4). This is the approach that has been adopted by the Swaziland Ministry of Education and Training. The Swaziland EDSEC policy presents inclusive education as an approach that includes and meets the needs of all learners regardless of their gender, stage of development, financial or any other circumstances (MoET, 2011). This notion is supported by (Engelbrecht, 2006; Miles & Singal, 2010). The EDSEC policy (2011, p. 12) further stipulates that

Inclusive education (IE) is concerned with the development and provision of quality education characterized by access and equity. It recognizes that every learner is unique and should be treated equitably by the teachers and the system. IE aims to serve the needs of all learners and enable them to reach their full potential, and seeks to involve parents and communities in this process.

Therefore the EDSEC policy in this case presents inclusive education as a cross-cutting approach that should inform and guide the education policy goal and strategies which follow and provide a principled guiding framework for the planning and coordination of EDSEC policy at every level from pre-primary to tertiary level. Inclusive Education is therefore viewed and recognized as an overarching checklist for strategic planning and implementation (MoET, 2011).

Reflecting on thinking and practice of inclusive education in Swaziland from 2011 onwards, the words 'access, meaningful participation and achievement' to one's maximum potential (Ainscow, 2006) best describe the understanding of inclusive education, notably these words are spelt out in the EDSEC policy. In essence access in this context can be about visibility of children with disabilities in ordinary schools. However, access in its literal sense is not a given considering that there are more layers of access which must be met for example, access to the physical structures in the school and to the curriculum. The latter being linked to meaningful participation in education which then leads to learner's achieving their maximum potential. This assertion is in line Article 26 of the Universal Declaration of Human Rights (United Nations, 1948) which defines the right to education as one of the fundamental rights of all humans. It is then the obligation of the Swaziland government and educational authorities to enable every Swazi citizen to have access to education and provide access in its literal sense. This aspect at the moment is very wanting but with time due to the progressive developments that are on-going in relation to IE in Swaziland, there is hope that eventually it will be realized.

In addition to this over the years, the understanding of inclusive education has evolved and now there are two more words that best describe it – 'equality and equity'. These thoughts are grounded in the social model and human rights view and are to the effect that every child matters, no child should be excluded from education and that school should provide learners with relevant quality education, regardless of their background, circumstances or ability. However, the author is aware of the multilateral and complex references these two words have in relation to inclusive education as noted in the UNESCO document Educational Equity and Public Policy: Comparison Results from 16 Countries (2007) that the term equity is subject to a variety of interpretations and "opinions diverge about what aspects of education should be distributed "equitably" to who and about what levels of disability are "equitable" or "inequitable" (p. 15). The same is reiterated in the above mentioned UNESCO document about access: "education access is the most basic equity concern because learning, regardless of the quality, cannot occur without access" (p. 23) as well as in the Policy Guidelines on Inclusion in Education (UNESCO, 2009). Nevertheless, education access has been an important component in the Swaziland understanding of inclusive education since 2010. This in evident in the 2014 Annual Education Census, which confirms that Swaziland has attained 97% net enrolments in primary education due to the simultaneous introduction of Free Primary Education and implementation of IE. However, the focus is now on ensuring 'quality', 'equality' and 'equity are achieved.

Furthermore this thinking is advanced by UNESCO, in a UNESCO Handbook on Education Policy Analysis and Programming (2013). The handbook highlights the relationship that exists between equity and access. It specifies that equity is an important aspect of education policy and the level of equity in the provision of education affects access to education and participation in education (p. 27). This is particularly important with regard to the question whether education services are provided equally to every student, paying special attention to the actual access and participation by different groups of learners. Earlier on, it was mentioned how learners with special needs and disabilities, were previously excluded and how they started to gain access to the mainstream school system from 2010. This development has continued and public schools in Swaziland now include a spectrum of students with various and multiple needs which schools are by law required to cater for. When access is expanded it has to be ensured that the level of participation and the quality of education do not fall short of basic quality standards. Equity in the Swaziland education system therefore includes the exploration of "whether education services are provided equally to all groups, and involves paying particular attention to the actual access and participation by sub-groups" (ibid., p. 27).

As indicated earlier, developments in IE from 2011 to date had to address perceptions anchored on IE as a marginal theme on how learners with disabilities can be included in mainstream schools instead of looking at how to transform the education system such that it responds to the diversity of learners, which is also the case in the majority (if not all) of the countries of the North. The tension in the 'specialised' and the 'inclusive' discourses in policymaking in Swaziland was evident in the existing policies, i.e. the 1999 National Policy Statement on Education which is aimed at increasing access to education for learners with special needs, in particular those with disabilities. Concepts on inclusion have developed from various ideas that include issues along the axis of both inclusion and exclusion. They therefore appear in various forms. This has not occurred in a linear way, as all these ideas can be active in one culture at the same time. Kozleski, Artiles, and Waitoller (2011) talk about waves of inclusive education based on "country's historical commitment to inclusive education and its attendant historical legacies about difference" (p. 7). The ideas and attitudes towards difference, diversity and inclusive education in Swaziland were further shaped by the author's exposure in the African Carribean Project (ACP) which was based on Capacity Building for Teachers on Inclusive Education. Four African countries, namely, Kenya, Uganda, Botswana and Swaziland and the UK were involved in the three (3) year capacity building project which started in 2009 and was completed in 2011. A Train the Trainer (ToT) model and programme content was developed by a university in London. This project provided a very rich forum to share ideas on inclusive education.

Some ideas have a greater impact on us than others and in the case of Swaziland, it was when the perspectives of the social and medical models or paradigms of disability were presented during the ACP project that a paradigm shift in perspective was realized. The social model perspectives were more consistent with the views of the EDSEC policy and therefore, Swaziland understanding sort of, developed from a narrow to broad understanding of inclusive education. In the process of development, part of the challenge was the continuing struggle with words, concepts, ideas and theories. This was a positive struggle in the sense that without it things would have been taken for granted and the move forward would not have occurred in the search for a better education for everyone. The toughest challenge was being critical of our own position as a country. This has been in particular with regards to how we use words, interpret ideas and in turn translate the words and ideas into practice. Without constant and critical reflection, we risked becoming so accustomed to our own ideas that we would not see or hear anything else. It is worth noting that international collaboration is important, so that as the colonized we have informed allies outside our own communities (Kincheloe & Steingberg, 2008).

Allan and Slee (2008) offer a discussion among researchers in inclusive education on the role of ideology in their researches and quote a colleague who said: "Ideology is like sweat: you can't smell your own" (p. 54). The same applies to how we use words and our awareness of this. When the educators went through training in the ACP project, the facilitators kept reminding them about the terms they use e.g. 'children with disabilities' which were used during the training. One of the modules in the training manual addressed the issue of perceptions, beliefs and attitudes towards certain groups of students and towards difference and diversity. The line of thought was that some of the words we use are counter-productive to the realisation of inclusive thinking and practice? This discussion had reference to how we determine and locate "difficulties" that students are considered to have. Historically, evidence indicates that students' difficulties are their problems – their inner characteristics – that need to be responded to, for example by categorisation and then, for example, special education. This approach is influenced by the medical approach towards learners which sees– the child – as the problem and implies the use of clinical methods to define student's special needs and thus "seeing students as diagnosable subjects assumes that they are in "need" of something – they are regarded as "defective". (Jóhannesson, 2006, p. 113).

An opposite view – which Swaziland adheres to since the ACP project – is to look at education through an inclusive lens which "implies a shift from seeing the child as the problem to seeing the education system as the problem" UNESCO, 2009, p. 14). The EDSEC subscribes to the social model which emphasizes the extent to which the physical, cultural, communication, attitudinal, transportation barriers in the environment serve every person and therefore the need to change (UNESCO, 2011). It is the responsibility of the system/the school to identify barriers and difficulties that students face and to respond to them by non-discriminating means with a focus on quality. This approach requires that we simultaneously explore exclusion as well – the grain of exclusion (Slee, 2014). Exclusion is another example of a concept that moved, developed and broadened the understanding of inclusive education in Swaziland. This line of understanding is influenced by Allan and Slee (2008) who note that: "Reducing educational exclusion and moving towards more inclusive futures for students disadvantaged by the complex interactions of poverty, disability, race, language, geographic location, sexuality and gender with pedagogy, curriculum and the organization of schooling is at the centre of our educational project" (p. 11). Exclusion is much more than the visible action of excluding someone from certain place or area. It has – as inclusion – references to all layers of the education system and moreover "in different societies different individuals and groups become more vulnerable and susceptible to exclusion" (Slee, 2011, p. 35). An inclusive approach to education requires that we constantly and critically explore the dominant culture of the school from the perspective of those who are somehow marginalized by the system.

5   Implementation and Positive Outcomes of Inclusive
      Education in Swaziland

In 2012, the Special Needs Unit in the Ministry of Education and Training embraced 'Inqaba' as a comprehensive inclusive school reform approach. Inqaba has provided new direction for developing comprehensive effective and sustainable programmes that improve access and empower schools to accommodate a broader range of learner's needs. Inclusive school development in

Swaziland is, therefore, situated within the context of a comprehensive larger school change effort that promises to improve educational outcomes for all learners whilst providing the necessary support so that general classrooms may be changed to accommodate a diverse range of learners. This policy direction confronts the issue of 'system change' and focuses on the extensive cultural shifts that must occur in the traditionally organised school to actualize inclusive education (Burrello, Sailor, & Kleinhammer-Tramill, 2013). It helps us to reflect deeply on the reforms that need to be made at policy level, in organizational and physical structures, roles and responsibilities of teachers, curriculum that is used in the classroom and the overall understanding of elements that are necessary for quality teaching and learning (Burello et al., 2013).

CSTL, internationally known as Child Friendly Schools (CFS), is a 2015 Southern African Development Community (SADC) framework which promotes child rights and child friendly programmes in schools. It was developed by SADC Member States to ensure holistic, comparable and sustainable care and support for teaching and learning of vulnerable learners throughout the region. The CSTL (Inqaba) framework is guided by six principles (SADC, 2015) which emphasize that addressing barriers to teaching and learning should be implemented in a systematic and holistic manner. The framework puts emphasis on access to quality education as a right for every child. It also promotes, protection, safety and psycho-social support to all children, particularly the most vulnerable (UNICEF, 2011). Inqaba is one effective and holistic reform approach that has potential to empower Swaziland schools to clearly define and commit themselves to genuine student learning which is essential to effective inclusive education development.

In practice, Swaziland's model of inclusive education can be described as a 'twin track approach' which requires cultivating and applying inclusive practices at all levels rather than concentrating solely on a child's impairment. As such the individual needs of children are addressed at the same time addressing societal, environmental, economic and political barriers to education. In this approach both special schools and regular schools provide education to every learner of school going age and this is supposed to be clear reflected in school development plans for each primary school. Producing inclusive policies suggests that the concept of inclusion would be imbedded within the various school development plans and permeates all policies in an effort to 'increase the learning and participation of all students' (Booth & Ainscow, 2002, p. 9, as cited in Amstrong, Amstrong, & Spandagou, 2012).

Meanwhile, the existence and effectiveness of special schools has been questioned by researchers, notably Lipsky and Gartner (1996). However, in the context of Swaziland, the existence and need to keep and develop special schools as resource centres to support inclusive education has been supported and advocated for as the best approach to meet the evolving needs of the country. Current provision of inclusive education ranges from special schools, inclusive classrooms, and resource centres in general education schools. This provision is further supported by the integration of inclusive pedagogy at pre-service and service teacher training. All teacher training institutions in Swaziland have pre-service and in-service teacher training programmes that incorporate inclusive education as a specific skill component. One institution has gone further to offer specialized training in special needs and inclusive education. Elder, Damiani, and Oswago (2015) argue that building teacher capacity is the basis for effective implementation of inclusive education. A Competency Based Curriculum has also been adopted by the Ministry of Education as a means to improve quality, equality and equity.

Inclusive education has also been harmonized with general education planning, and policies towards and understanding of inclusion (UNESCO, 2011). A comprehensive national strategy, namely, the 'National Education and Training Improvement Programme (NETIP) was put in place in November 2014 (2nd revised version) for the implementation of the EDSEC policy. The NETIP clearly articulates the education sector's activities geared towards providing an equitable and inclusive education system for all Swazi citizens within a three year term period 2013–2016. Budgetary support, action frameworks, indicators and implementation commitments have been included in the NETIP and a sub-subsequent monitoring and evaluation plan for NETIP. The NETIP has been used as a base for budget allocation for SEN and also for sourcing financial resources from development partners. For example, beginning 2016, a non-government organization supported the development of a strategy for early identification of children with disabilities. Provision of a clear and consistent framework for the identification, assessment and support required to enable every child to flourish in mainstream learning environment (UNICEF, 2011) is a priority in the NETIP.

6 Tensions and Key Challenges

Given that inclusive education was given impetus by an international declaration at the International Conference on SEN in Salamanca in 1994, it is accepted that the term 'inclusive education', and indeed 'inclusion' in educational terms, has been associated with SEN. As this association necessitates that we constantly and critically explore the dominant culture of special classes, special treatment by teachers, specialist teachers etc, and inclusive education is inherently faced by tensions. This association continues to cause tension in the field and challenged shifts in thinking as well as developments towards focusing on a wider agenda for inclusion rather narrowly being concerned only with learners categorized as having special educational needs and/or disability (Dyson et al., 2004 cited in Ainscow, Booth, & Dyson, 2006; Clough, 1996). The belief that some learners are 'uneducable' or belong in special schools has contributed to tensions in the field. Teachers believe students with disabilities have a right to be in regular schools and receive quality education but "there are oppositional ideas installed through historical engagement with international thinking around the need for specialist support and this continues to be reinforced by the continued focus on specialist, 'expert' knowledge" (Pather, 2006, p. 12).

The debate on 'full inclusion' and deficit approach where the type and severity is used as a measure to determine access to a regular or special school setting continues to create tensions within the Swaziland education sector. The UN Standard Rules on Equalization of Opportunities for Persons with Disability (UN, 1993, Rule 22) presents that special schools may be considered where ordinary schools cannot make adequate provision (UN Standard Rules on Equalization of Opportunities for Persons with Disability – UN, 1993, Rule 6 of 22). Yet the UN Convention on the Rights of Persons with Disabilities focuses on inclusive education system and therefore questions the 'necessity' of a segregated special education system.

The reliance on external assessment results to assess good schools is influencing schools not to accept learners who will not help them meet the target of being to be in the top 10. There are contradictions in terms of how we define achievement for learners – we still use pass or fail and not competences to define achievement. Furthermore, the reality is that while social policy is dominated by the rhetoric of inclusion, the reality for many remains one of exclusion. The language of special education continues to impede analysis of deep seated problems in respect to both funding and policy for improving quality of education for all children. Slee (1995, p. 31) observed that 'new language policy is easily learned and accommodated, but it is more problematic for this to penetrate the fine-grain of organizational curriculum and pedagogy. This is because, though the implications of the policies are grasped well, they clash with more fundamental beliefs and values. Legal frameworks, which, in theory have created the opportunity and means to claim rights, will not, on their own challenge the deep seated discriminatory practices which still subsist thus delaying the much anticipated change (UNESCO, 2011). Measures are therefore needed to build more capacity of the education system as a whole in order to challenge inequity and meet the obligations.

A shift in thinking has been observed amongst educators, in particular, teachers who have had direct experience with inclusive education. The more teachers are involved in inclusive education the more they gain understanding on the broader perspective of inclusion. Research suggests that teachers who have the most positive attitude towards inclusive education are those that have direct experience with inclusive education (Mittler, 2012). Continued capacity building at pre and in-service levels and embracing Inqaba also contributes positively to addressing this tension. Building teacher capacity and experiences with inclusion is the basis for positive attitudinal change (Elder, Damiani, & Oswago, 2015).

7   Conclusion

This chapter has reflected on the developments that have shaped the current situation regarding inclusive education in Swaziland. Swaziland has learnt from other countries and further considered the context and reality when developing the 2011 education and training policy and strategy to transform the education system towards inclusion. The author argues that the holistic approach adopted by Swaziland towards policy development and implementation of inclusive education is considered a more sustainable approach to inclusive education development in Swaziland, and perhaps offers an example of a possible approach for other countries within and outside the African region. Given that inclusive education is an evolutionary, rather than a revolutionary process, it should be everybody's business (Slee, 2011; Rogers, 2012) to minimize inequalities and exclusionary practices in education. The Inqaba approach presents such an opportunity to have everyone involved in minimizing exclusionary practices in the Swaziland education system.

However, going forward, there is still need for a sector wide approach to continuous debates around the following questions: What does it really mean to have an education system that is inclusive? Who needs inclusion and why? (Armstrong et al., 2012). This chapter highlighted that inclusion "... involves all students" (Ballard, 1997, p. 244 as cited by Berhanu, 2011). What educational practices is it contesting, what common values is it advocating and by what criteria should it be judged? There are also struggles over purposes of education – is it just about doing academic subjects, passing external examinations and qualifying to go to University. How can Competency Based curriculum promote inclusion of every learner in the system? Swaziland also needs to adopt a more holistic view of student assessment that considers academic, behavioural, social and emotional aspects of rather than just academic achievement. Careful thought by all education practitioners around these questions will further enhance implementation of inclusive education from a Swaziland context.

References

African Charter on the Rights and Welfare of the Child. (1999).

Ainscow, M. (1999). *Understanding the development of inclusive school.* London: Falmer Press.

Ainscow, M. (2006). The next step for special education. *British Journal of Special Education, 27*(2), 76–80.

Ainscow, M. (2007). Taking an inclusive turn. *Journal of Research in Special Educational Needs, 7*(1), 3–7.

Ainscow, M., Booth, T., & Dyson, A. (2006). Inclusion and the standards agenda: Negotiating policy pressures in England. *International Journal of Inclusive Education, 10*(4–50), 295–308.

Allan, J., & Slee, R. (2008). *Doing inclusive education research.* Rotterdam, The Netherlands: Sense Publishers.

Armstrong, A. C., Armstrong, D., & Spandagou, I. (2010). *Inclusive education: International policy and practice.* London: Sage Publications.

Balescut, J., & Eklindh, K. (2006). *Literacy and persons with developmental disabilities: Why and how?* (Background paper prepared for the education for all global monitoring report 2006 literacy for life). Paris: UNESCO.

Ballard, K. (Ed.). (1998). *Inclusive education: International voices on disability and justice.* London: Falmer Press.

Barton, L. (1997). Inclusive education: Romantic, subversive or realistic? *International Journal of Inclusive Education, 1*(3), 231–242.

Berhanu, G. (2011). Inclusive education in Sweden: Responses, challenges and prospects, university of Gothenburg. *International Journal of Special Education, 26*(2), 125–145.

Booth, T. (2005). Keeping the future alive: Putting inclusive values into action. *FORUM, 47*(2–3), 150–158.

Booth, T., & Ainscow, M. (Eds.). (1998). *From them to us: An international study of inclusion in education.* London: Routledge.

Central Statistics Office. (2007). *National census.* Mbabane: Central Statistical Office.

Elder, B. C., Damiani, M., & Oswago, B. (2015). From attitudes to practice: Using inclusive teaching strategies in Kenyan primary schools. *International Journal of Inclusive Education, 20*(4), 1–22. Retrieved from http://dx.doi.org/10.1080/13603116.2015.1082648

Engelbrecht, P. (2006). The implementation of inclusive education in South Africa after ten years of democracy. *European Journal of Psychology of Education, XXI*, 253–264.

Holt, L. (2003). (Dis)abling children in primary school micro-spaces: Geographies of inclusion and exclusion. *Health & Place, 9*, 119–128.

Johannesson, I. A. (2006). Concepts of teacher knowledge as social strategies. *Pedagogy, Culture & Society, 14*(1) 19–34. doi:10.1080/14681360500487520

Kincheloe, J., Burrello, L., Sailor, W., & Kleinhammer-Tramill, J. (2013). *Unifying educational systems*. New York, NY: Routledge.

Kozelski, E. B., Artiles, A. J., Fletcher, T., & Engelbrecht, P. (2009). Understanding the dialects of the local and global in education for all: A comparative case study. *International Critical Childhood Policy Studies, 2*(1), 15–19.

Kozleski, E. B., Artiles, A. J., & Waitoller, F. R. (2011). Introduction: Equity in inclusive education. Historical trajectories and theoretical commitments. In A. J. Artiles, E. B. Kozleski, & F. R. Waitoller (Eds.), *Inclusive education. Examining equity on five continents* (pp. 1–14). Cambridge, MA: Harvard Education Press.

Lipsky, D. K., & Garner, A. (1996). Inclusion, school restructuring and the remaking of American society. *Harvard Educational Review, 66*(4), 762–797.

Miles, S., & Singal, N. (2010). The education for all inclusive education debate: Conflict, contradiction or opportunity? *International Journal of Inclusive Education, 14*, 1–15.

Mittler, P. (2012). *Working towards inclusive education: Social contexts*. New York, NY: David Fulton Publishers.

Pather, S. (2006). Demystifying inclusion: Implications for sustainable inclusive practice. *International Journal of Inclusive Education, 11*(5–6), 627–643.

Pather, S., & Nxumalo, C. P. (2013). Challenging understanding of inclusive education policy development in Southern Africa through comparative reflection. *International Journal of Inclusive Education, 17*(4), 420–434.

Rogers, C. (2012). Inclusive education, exclusion and difficult difference: A call for humanity? *British Journal of Sociology of Education, 33*(3), 475–485.

SADC. (2015). *Policy framework on care and support for teaching and learning*.

Slee, R. (2006). Limits to and possibilities for educational reform. *International Journal of Inclusive Education, 10*(2–3), 109–119.

Slee, R. (2011). *The irregular school. Exclusion, schooling and inclusive education.* London & New York, NY: Routledge.

Spurgeon, W. (2007). Diversity and choice for children with complex needs. In R. Cigman (Ed.), *Included or excluded? The challenge of the mainstream for some SEN children.* London: Routledge.

Steinberg, S. (2008). Indigenous knowledges in education: Complexities, dangers, and profound benefits. In N. K. Denzin, Y. S. Lincoln, & L. T. Smith (Eds.), *Handbook of critical and indigenous methodologies* (pp. 135–156). Thousand Oaks, CA: Sage Publications.

The Government of the Kingdom of Swaziland. (2011). *The Swaziland education and training sector policy.* Mbabane: Ministry of Education and Training.

The Kingdom of Swaziland. (1972). *Imbokodvo national manifesto.*

UNESCO. (1994). *The Salamanca statement and framework for action on special needs education, world conference on special needs education.* Paris: UNESCO.

UNESCO. (2003a). *Overcoming exclusion through inclusive approaches in education a challenge a vision conceptual paper.* Paris: UNESCO.

UNESCO. (2003b). *Open file on inclusive education: Support materials for managers and administrators.* Paris: UNESCO.

UNESCO. (2005). *Guidelines for inclusion. Ensuring access to education for all.* Paris: UNESCO.

UNESCO. (2007). *Educational equity and public policy: Comparison results from 16 countries.* Paris: UNESCO.

UNESCO, (2009). *Key principles for promoting quality in inclusive education.* Paris: UNESCO.

UNESCO. (2013). *Handbook on education policy analysis and programming.* Paris: UNESCO.

UNICEF. (2011). *The right of children with disabilities to education: A rights-based approach to inclusive education.* Geneva: UNICEF Regional Office for Central and Eastern Europe and the Commonwealth of Independent States (CEECIS).

United Nations. (2006). *Convention on the rights of persons with disabilities.* Retrieved from http://www.un.org/disabilities/convention/conventionfull.shtml

United Nations. (2009). *Some facts about persons with disabilities.* Retrieved from http://www.un.org/disabilities/convention/facts.shtml

United Nations. (2015). *Transforming our world: The 2030 agenda for sustainable development.* Retrieved from https://sustainabledevelopment.un.org/post2015/transformingourworld

United Nations Educational, Scientific and Cultural Organization (UNESCO). (2005). *Guidelines for inclusion: Ensuring access to education for all.* Retrieved from http://unesdoc.unesco.org/images/0014/001402/140224e.pdf

United Nations Educational, Scientific and Cultural Organization (UNESCO). (2009). *Policy guidelines on inclusive education.* Retrieved from http://unesdoc.unesco.org/images/0017/001778/177849e.pdf

CHAPTER 9

Challenges of Implementing Inclusive Education and Supporting Marginalized Groups in Ethiopia

Ali Sani Side

1   Introduction

Modern education started in Ethiopia in 1908 and the contribution of missionaries from different corners of the globe is invaluable for the education of children with disabilities particularly for the education of blind, deaf and intellectual disabilities. Ethiopia also signed the different international conventions to support the education and life of people with disabilities. The commitment also manifested in different ways like making the issues a concern of the Federal constitution of the country, including in the education policy, preparing special needs education strategy and many other inclusive education related initiatives. However, still only a few people with disabilities are practically benefiting considering the population of Ethiopia (Ethiopia has over 100 million population). Implementation of inclusive education from policy into practice is still not a reality. This chapter highlights some of the challenges.

2   Carrier Structure

The Federal democratic republic of Ethiopia has nine regional administration regions (Tigray, Amhara, Benishangul, Somali, Gambela, SNPPR, Oromia, Harari and Afar) and two city administrations (Addis Ababa and Dire Dawa). Of the nine regions, four of them namely Afar, Somali, Benishangulgumz and Gambela are emerging regions. The government of Ethiopia gives special attention to these regions because their development is significantly lower in terms of infrastructure, education, health, agriculture and draught stricken areas. Each region or city administration has administration structures down to the school level, from Federal government to Regional administration to Zonal administration, Woreda administration, Kebele administration and then schools. The number of zones, woredas and schools vary across regions as per the population size and land coverage.

© KONINKLIJKE BRILL NV, LEIDEN, 2019 | DOI:10.1163/9789004391505_010

At Federal level, the Ministry of Education of Ethiopia is organized under three wings; General Education, TVET and Higher Education. There are 34 directorate offices under the three wings and 11 are under general education. Special Support and inclusive Education directorate is one of the eleven directorate offices under general education. The directorate office is responsible for two major tasks; providing comprehensive support to the four emerging regions (Afar, Somali, Benishangul and Gambela) and running inclusive education programs in the country. However, the first task seems more sensitive to government and highly politicized than inclusive education. As a result, inclusive education in reality is overlooked. Implementation of inclusive education in the country is not a priority despite the government being a signatory to many international conventions. For example, one of the challenges facing implementation of inclusive education in Ethiopia is lack of clear carrier structure. At Federal level, there are only four experts of special needs education who are supposed to support regions across the country but at regional and city administration levels, there is only one focal person responsible for inclusive education. In some regions like Afar, the focal person is responsible for managing other cross cutting issues like HIV/AIDS and school feeding program. Hence, there is no consistent carrier structure existing at each level all the way from federal to school level and there is no formal structure for accountability. The problem relating to job descriptions for each level has been resolved by the Ethiopian Special Needs Professional Association very recently in 2017.

3   Teacher Training in Ethiopia

Teachers are crucial in determining what happens in classrooms and there are those who would argue that the development of more inclusive classrooms requires teachers to cater for different student learning needs through the modification or differentiation of the curriculum (Forlin, 2004, as cited in Rouse, 2008). However, the way teachers get trained in Ethiopia for inclusive education is another challenge the country has been facing. Teachers get training in two modalities in Ethiopia; in service and regular. For the first modality, teachers already hired by public schools attend college and University courses from July to August for three consecutive years because primary and secondary school children take breaks for the new academic year whereas for the second modality, prospective teachers take college and University courses regularly from September to June for three years. There are 38 colleges and only ten of them have specialized departments for special needs education where all the students take different inclusive education related courses and very few skill courses for three years. On the other hand, all students enrolling in other departments are expected to take three credit (48 hours) course entitled "Introduction to Special Needs Education", This is more of a medical model and deficit focused course. With the support of the government of Finland, Ethiopia amended the course to focus on the social model and it is only from 2017 on that the course is entitled "Inclusive Education in Ethiopian Primary Schools".

There are 43 public Universities in the country and ten of them have a department for special needs education at first degree level. However, regardless of the level of the degree, theoretical and conceptual issues are more dominant than action oriented interventions in the courses. Many of diploma level graduates cannot sign and communicate with deaf students, cannot read and write Braille, and lack skills to practically apply the different behavior intervention packages. Ethiopia signed international legal frameworks to show commitment for the realization of inclusive education. However, the commitment appears more on paper than in action at grassroots level. As a result, discrepancy is happening between the ambition of school leaders towards realizing inclusive education and the skills and knowledge teachers are actually equipped with. For example, unpublished master's degree study thesis conducted by Demisew (2014) in Addis Ababa on inclusive education practices of primary schools, presents the conflicting response of a school director and school teacher regarding a question about helping children with special needs in schools with necessary skills. The director says that:

> In order to support the SWDS/SWSN effectively, teachers should have additional skills, and knowledge like Braille reading and writing, mobility and orientation, and sign language. (p. 61)

A teacher argued that he had no opportunity to learn the skills so that he could not support students with special educational needs saying:

> I don't understand Braille, sign language and related materials at all, I am telling the truth, I did not get a chance to get the trainings on skills to support students with special educational needs. (p. 61)

Teachers should be building upon positive attitudes because without positive attitude and values, it has no meaning to talk about skills. The appropriate training of mainstream teachers is crucial if they are to be confident and competent in teaching children with diverse educational needs. The principles of inclusion should be built into teacher training programmes, which should be about attitudes and values not just knowledge and skills (WHO, 2011).

According to the Education Sector Development programme V (2015), 800 resource centers (Inclusive education support centers) will be established from 2015/2016–2019/2020. The Federal Ministry of Education, Ethiopia has also prepared guideline for establishing and managing inclusive education/ support centers (2015). The guideline explains that:

> Itinerant teachers should be certified SNE teachers preferably at BA (First Degree) level. In addition to what is listed in their duties and responsibilities, these teachers are expected to visit satellite schools once or twice a week which magnifies that their task is highly demanding. (pp. 18–19)

The guideline listed responsibilities of Itinerant teachers. It states that, they get additional incentives for the additional responsibilities they carry out. Contrary to this, prospective SNE teachers take no course(s) at universities or colleges on the role of the itinerant teachers and there is no carrier structure defined for itinerant teachers by the government. Itinerant Teachers are appointed without special training for this role. The guideline was published in 2015 but there is no incentive for these teachers at all. They get paid like any other teachers despite the guideline's claim that the job they are expected to engage is, is demanding by its nature. There are 32,048 primary schools in Ethiopia (ESDP V, 2015) and only sixteen model inclusive resource centers have been established by the Ministry of Education (MoE), with the support of funding from the government of Finland from 2013 to 2017. Of course different regions established their own resource centers although there is no official report on the number and quality of these centers. However, the assumption is that itinerant teachers reach out to all satellite schools surrounding their resource centers and support schools who include students with special educational needs. Ethiopia is a very vast country in terms of area coverage and schools are far from each other so itinerant teachers experience difficulty travelling to satellite schools once or twice a week as per the recommendation of the guideline.

Generally, except teachers specializing in special needs education, all other teachers take only one course related to special needs education or inclusive education at colleges or University, which less likely makes them ready to understand and support children with special educational needs. Teachers specializing in SNE also lack basic skills to support deaf, blind, Deaf-blind and other students. In addition, teachers who are good with Braille, sign language, orientation and mobility and behavior management skills do not get refresher courses to update them with new knowledge in the area.

Filling these gaps relating to training may facilitate the movement towards inclusive education at practical level more quickly. Rouse (2008) supports this notion, suggesting:

> There is widespread support for inclusion at a philosophical level, there are some concerns that the policy of inclusion is difficult to implement because teachers are not sufficiently well prepared and supported to work in inclusive ways. Inclusion requires teachers to accept the responsibility for creating schools in which all children can learn and feel they belong. In this task, teachers are crucial because of the central role they play in promoting participation and reducing underachievement, particularly with children who might be perceived as having difficulties in learning. (p. 1)

4   Lack of Awareness

A country's commitment to inclusive education is beyond showing agreement to the international community working in the area. It requires understanding the philosophy and how to move this on practically. According to IDDC (1998; cited in Mitiku et al., 2014), a limited understanding of the concept of disability, negative attitudes towards persons with disabilities and a hardened resistance to change are the major barriers impeding inclusive education. This seems true in Ethiopia because socially influential individuals, authorities, religious people and majority of school communities have limitations about understanding inclusion and disability itself. Hence, prominent figures are less likely be seen raising awareness about inclusion to influence government in accommodating more people with disabilities in work spaces and socially. The author of this chapter has completed a situation analysis for the development of an inclusive education Master plan for Ethiopia from 2016–2025 and found out that demand of awareness raising program on inclusive education and disability is one of the priorities. Regions and city administrations in Ethiopia requested this to be considered by the Federal Ministry of Education, Ethiopia. A study by Mitiku et al. (2014) also indicated that, despite the different opportunities Ethiopia has for inclusive education, a lack of awareness, commitment and collaboration are challenges.

Furthermore, differences among professionals of special needs education in the country on concepts and definition of terms are also a key challenge. It is common hearing "inclusion experts" using special needs education, inclusive education and integrated education interchangeably. Citing UNESCO-commissioned report on Education for All, Franck (2013) states that Ethiopia utilizes the terms 'special needs education' and 'inclusive education' as one concept, defined as 'focus[ing] on children and students who are at risk of repetition and drop-out due to learning difficulties, disabilities, socio-emotional problems, or are excluded from education'. According to Lewis (2009, as cited in Franck, 2013), there are a myriad of definitions for inclusive education, integrated education and special needs education, leading to different interpretations in policy language and implementation. Solving the differences in understanding basics about inclusive education and special needs education among professionals in the area and adapting or creating context specific definition for basic terms in inclusion needs academic discourse in the country. Moreover, the gap in aware-ness among professionals in other fields of study, community leaders, influential figures and all other stakeholders is a challenge Ethiopia has to deal with.

5 Curriculum Modification

Learners must meet curriculum objectives in order to pass a certain level of education. Objectives, content, learning experiences, resources and assess-ment need to be considered well in the curriculum (MoE, 2012). With that in mind, the MoE in Ethiopia has prepared guidelines for curriculum differen-tiation and an Individual Education program in 2012 for children with special educational needs. The guideline for curriculum differentiation and Individual education program (2012) explains differentiated curriculum as:

> an adapted and modified type of curriculum that focuses on ability level of learners. It aligns the cognitive, affective, communicative, and physical demands of the formal curriculum to the capacities, strengths and needs of individual learners. (p. 12)

The definition for the differentiated curriculum is well articulated in the guide-line and it further elaborates the importance for teachers to adapt and modify the formal and regular curriculum to meet the specific learning needs of stu-dents with special educational needs. It also suggests for teachers to breakdown subject content into manageable parts without worrying about time factor.

On review of the guidelines, several questions need to be asked:

– Do teachers really breakdown subject matters to make the lessons suit to students with special educational needs?
– Do they give more time for students with special educational needs during lesson delivery and assessment?
– Do they even try to adapt or modify the regular curriculum for students with special educational needs?

154   SIDE

Based on experience and understanding of local practice, the answers to these questions would be NO. For example, many of the text books and reference materials are not transcribed into Braille for blind students particularly for secondary education level (from grade 9–12). Deaf students usually do not get sign language translators during lesson delivery and other discussion sessions. Many children with invisible challenges like children with learning difficulties are not identified at all so that they do not get additional educational support. Therefore, curriculum adaptation and modification to the needs and ability of learners is a challenge Ethiopia has not yet resolved.

6   Lack and Shortage of Assistive Devices

Many of the challenges emanating from inaccessible physical environments can be countered by the use of disability assistive devices. The devices can make life simple for people with disability and help to prevent additional impairment. Moreover, assistive devices are one of the key elements in order to advance inclusion. According to WHO (2015):

> Assistive devices and technologies are those whose primary purpose is to maintain or improve an individual's functioning and independence to facilitate participation and to enhance overall well-being. They can also help prevent impairments and secondary health conditions. Examples of assistive devices and technologies include wheelchairs, prostheses, hearings aids, visual aids, and specialized computer software and hardware that increase mobility, hearing, vision, or communication capacities. In many low-income and middle-income countries, only 5–15% of people who require assistive devices and technologies have access to them.

A shortage of assistive devices is one of the challenges problems in Ethiopia. Some regions report that many of the devices are unaffordable and other low tech devices are not easily accessible. Even special needs professionals do not understand types of assistive technologies/devices and consider these luxury instead of basics for people with disabilities. For example, protective headgear for people with epilepsy, a pressure relief cushion to protect wheelchair users with paralysis from pressure sores and associated fatal infections, ramps with handrails for children with physical impairment, and parallel bars for people who have challenges with balance and strength. The latter is not easily accessible to purchase in Ethiopia unless imported from abroad. In addition, technological devices that could enhance the performance of people with disabilities like screen readers, computer software, hearing aids and other are not easily available in local markets and affordable if they are available.

7   Accessibility

Ethiopia has a building code under proclamation No. 624/2009. This obliges any kind of construction to be disability considerate. However, very few buildings in Addis Ababa have physical accessibility to people with motor disability. A significant portion of government owned buildings are not physically accessible, except Hawassa University (one of the 43 public Universities in the country). All public Universities have no ramp to the first floor. The common answer for why do universities not have ramps or lifts to higher floors is that "students with orthopedic impairments can get services at ground level room". This is the violation of the rights of students with disabilities granted in the country higher education proclamation No. 650/2009. The proclamation section three article 40, sub article from 1–4 states that:

1. Institutions shall make, to the extent possible, their facilities and programmes amenable to use with relative ease by physically challenged students.
2. Institutions shall, to the extent that situations and resources permit, relocate classes, develop alternative testing procedures, and provide different educational auxiliary aids in the interest of students with physical challenges.
3. Building designs, campus physical landscape, computers and other infrastructures of institutions shall take into account the interests of physically challenged students.
4. Institutions shall ensure that students with physical challenges get to the extent necessary and feasible academic assistance, including tutorial sessions, exam time extensions and deadline extensions.

With that in mind, the proclamation disregards students with other disabilities except "physically challenged". Due to this, students with different disabilities categories show interest to join universities like Addis Ababa, Bahirdar, Hawassa and Dilla universities. However, no accessibility to physical environments prevents them from enrolling. The social environment is more difficult than the physical environment in schools and a key factor to implementing inclusive education. As is discussed under lack of disability awareness, there is a misconception about people with disability and disability itself. Generally, more accessible physical and social environments for students with special educational needs is a challenge in Ethiopia.

References

Demisew, A. (2014). *Inclusive education practices of primary schools in Yeka sub city* (Unpublished master's thesis). Addis Ababa University, Addis Ababa.

Franck, B. (2013). *Inclusive education and children with disabilities in Ethiopia.* Denver: Education and Development University of Denver.

Ministry of Education. (2012). *Guideline for curriculum differentiation and individual education program.* Addis Ababa: Ministry of Education.

Ministry of Education. (2015). *Education sector development programmes V.* Addis Ababa: Ministry of Education.

Ministry of Education. (2015). *Guideline for establishing and managing inclusive education resources/support centers.* Addis Ababa: Ministry of Education.

Rouse, M. (2008). Developing inclusive practice: A role for teachers and teacher education. *Journal Education in the North, 16*(1), 6–13.

The Federal Negarit Gazeta. (2009). *Ethiopian building proclamation no. 624/2009.* Addis Ababa: The Federal Negarit Gazeta.

The Federal Negarit Gazeta. (2009). *Higher education proclamation no. 650/2009.* Addis Ababa: The Federal Negarit Gazeta.

Wondwosen, M., Yitayal, A., & Semahegn, M. (2014). Challenges and opportunities to implement inclusive education. *Asian Journal of Humanity, Art and Literature, 1*(2), 118.

World Health Organization. (2011). *Assistive technology for children with disabilities: Creating opportunities for education, inclusion and participation.* Geneva: World Health Organization.

World Health Organization. (2011). *World report on disability.* Retrieved from http://www.who.int/about/licensing/copyright_form/enindex.html

Printed in the United States
By Bookmasters